Key Stage 3
Classbook

Letts
EDUCATIONAL

English

for September 2000

John
Green

First published 1998
Second edition 2000

Reprinted 1998 (twice)

Letts Educational
Schools and Colleges Division
9–15 Aldine Street
London W12 8AW
Tel 020 8740 2266
Fax 020 8743 8451

Text: © John Green 1998

Design and illustrations © (Letts Educational) Ltd 1998

Design and page layout: Ken Vail Graphic Design, Cambridge

Illustrations: Sylvie Poggio Artists Agency (Nick Duffy, Rosalind Hudson, Paul McCaffrey, Phil Smith and Sarah Warburton)

Colour reproduction by PDQ Repro Ltd, Bungay, Suffolk

Picture research by Brooks Krikler Research

British Library Cataloguing-in-Publication Data

A CIP record for this book is available from the British Library

ISBN 1 84085 416 2

Printed and Bound in Spain

Letts Educational Limited, a division of Granada Learning Limited.
Part of the Granada Media Group.

Acknowledgements

The author and publishers gratefully acknowledge permission to reproduce the following copyright material: pp. 24–6 (text) approximately 420 words (pp. 142–144) from *Joby* by Stan Barstow (Michael Joseph, 1964) copyright © 1964 by Stan Barstow, reproduced by permission of Penguin Books Ltd; pp. 34–5 (text) approximately 235 words (p. 117) from *The Kingdom by the Sea: A Journey Around the Coast of Great Britain* by Paul Theroux (Hamish Hamilton, 1983) copyright © Paul Theroux, 1983, reproduced by permission of Penguin Books Ltd; pp. 94–5 (text) Jacky Smith/Homes & Gardens/Robert Harding Syndication; pp. 96–7 from *The Rough Guide to Italy*, Rough Guides; pp. 107–110 (text) from *Our Day Out* © Willy Russell, reproduced by permission of the publisher, Methuen Publishing Ltd; pp. 132–5 (text) approx 1200 words (pp. 47–51) from *Basketball Game* by Julius Lester (Kestrel, 1974) copyright © Julius Lester 1972; pp. 188–90 (text) from *Things Fall Apart* © Chinua Achebe, reproduced by permission of the publisher, Heinemann Educational; pp. 202–203 by kind permission of WWF–UK (World Wide Fund For Nature); pp. 204–5 (text) from *Howards End* by E. M. Forster, reproduced by permission of The Provost and Scholars of Kings College, Cambridge, and The Society of Authors as the Literary Representatives of the E. M. Forster Estate; pp. 230–1 (text) extracted from *Notes from a Small Island*, © Bill Bryson 1995, published by Black Swan, a division of Transworld Publishers, all rights reserved; p. 245 from *Oranges from Spain* by kind permission of the author, David Park.

The author and publishers are grateful to the following for permission to reproduce photographs: Corbis: pages 132, 133, 134; Mary Evans Pictrue Library: 147; Eye Ubquitous: 24, 50; Ronald Grant Archive: 205; Kobal Collection: 55; © National Gallery, London: 230; Rex Features: 48, 110, 186; Spectrum Colour Library: 231; Frank Spooner Pictures: 34, 48; Tony Stone/Getty Images: 15, 33, 41, 66, 68, 93 all, 171, 200, 219; Trip Photo Library: 94; Roger Vlitos: 4.

Contents

Introduction

Units

Introduction to the second edition

This Classbook has proved so popular with teachers that it has been necessary to produce a second edition that takes account of changes in the recently revised National Curriculum Orders for English. However, the changes have not been radical and extensive – the original intention of the book was to provide teachers and pupils with learning support and skills practice as they worked through the programmes of study, and that material is still entirely relevant. Teachers may revise their schemes of work, but the basic understanding and skills remain the same. The one aspect of the National Curriculum Orders that does receive additional emphasis is ICT, and some attempt has been made in this second edition to give support in this area.

English teachers have made increasing use in recent years of computer word processing facilities to support pupils in their written work. Such facilities make text manipulation – from simple cut-and-paste to more sophisticated techniques – more manageable for many pupils. The additional support of built-in spell-checking/grammar/thesaurus devices has encouraged those with specific problems, and pupils with handwriting difficulties have been pleased to overcome such 'presentational' handicaps and produce work that looks attractive. Even 'clip-art' has its contribution to make as pupils become more adept at understanding, handling and creating non-fiction texts such as advertisements, news bulletins and leaflets. This whole range of possibilities is increasingly supported and extended by desktop publishing programmes designed specially for use in schools.

Further, teachers and pupils are increasingly making use of ICT for 'research' and to seek out information that previously would have been discovered in the school library. Computer encyclopaedias and many other texts are now freely available on CD and may be accessed far more rapidly than the traditional search for (and through) reference books – although this is not to say that such skills are redundant or that books should be accorded second-class status. Nevertheless, it has to be admitted that the Internet offers a global range of information that has never previously been available to pupils.

Pupils not only have access through ICT to many sources of information. Computer databases also allow them to manipulate and present information – for example, results compiled from classroom surveys – in different and interesting ways. This sort of data manipulation may be a point of contact for cross-curricular links – say, with maths – but means that pupils may, simply at the touch of a key, consider the information they have gathered from a number of different perspectives; and, at the same time, examine the effects and implications of the perspective from which that information is presented.

Finally, many pupils, in their private lives now communicate using e-mail, which has become a genre in its own right. It seems appropriate to consider the characteristics of this new genre as well as of other 'electronic' text types – Internet texts, and so on – from the point of view of their language, structure and conventions in the same way as more traditional text forms are analysed, understood and created.

Opportunities for all these sorts of activities are noted at appropriate points throughout the book, because this second edition is intended to provide all the support of the previous version – 'nowt taken out'! – but with the extra support in the field of ICT that is necessary for teaching and learning in the new millennium.

This sign indicates optional ICT exercises.

Introduction

The scope and purpose of this book

This is intended to be a textbook in the traditional sense, providing teachers and pupils with a course book which offers a framework for covering the requirements of the programmes of study in the National Curriculum for English at Key Stage 3.

Activities for the three attainment target areas – Speaking and listening, Reading and Writing – will be integrated within each of the 21 units of work.

Each unit consists of the following elements:

- an oral activity – related to the central text or skills focus of the unit
- questions – to test comprehension, including questions that focus on the way meaning and structure contribute to understanding and response
- learning about language – focusing on the terminology of grammar and literary criticism
- word building – examining the way words are built up, their derivation and the rules that govern spelling
- text building – looking at the grammar and structure of sentences, paragraphs and 'whole texts', and the way punctuation supports clarity of meaning
- skills practice – including a range of exercises to reinforce learning and understanding
- writing – providing pupils with the opportunity to use newly acquired skills to improve the quality of their own writing and to practise writing for different purposes and in different styles.

The programmes of study for Key Stages 3 and 4 are not presented separately in the National Curriculum and so inevitably there has been some selectivity in content: for example, the analysis of literary techniques of a more advanced type such as setting, period and timeshift have been omitted as more appropriate to a Key Stage 4/GCSE course.

How to use this book

The 21 units of work are designed to give a framework for learning in Years 7, 8 and 9: approximately eight units, two or three per term for Year 7, another eight for Year 8, and the remainder for Year 9 (where additional material will be needed for test preparation). For many pupils, some of the earlier units will provide useful revision opportunities for checking skills that have already been mastered at Key Stage 2 and offer 'reference points' for correcting errors at later stages.

Working together

This book is not intended to be an alternative to well organised and effective teaching. The classroom interchange between teacher and pupil is absolutely central to successful learning and this book should be used as a tool, with teacher and pupils working through it together.

It is not a 'teach yourself' book for pupils to use on their own without guidance; no one textbook could hope to cater for the individual needs of every pupil. However, many of the exercises will provide useful homework tasks that pupils can work through independently to reinforce what has been learned in class.

Speaking and listening

The introductory oral activities provide a starting point for each unit, but teachers will want to shape these according to the needs of their pupils and what is appropriate to their own classroom situation. Oral work always needs to be well structured and controlled and teachers will have their individual methods of interpreting the suggestions given in ways that are most helpful to their own pupils.

Furthermore, the activities are intended mainly to focus on aspects of the learning content of the unit. They will need to be restructured to suit individual requirements if used for assessment purposes, with task, assessment objectives and performance criteria clearly integrated – and made explicit to pupils to encourage self-evaluation.

Some aspects of Speaking and listening work – for example, the use of gesture and intonation and participation in drama – are given little emphasis in this book. This is because such work involves 'practical' activities which teachers will find easier to organise during the study of full plays and playscripts rather than using extracts, which is all the scope of this book allows.

Similarly, little space is given to work on accent and dialect because such aspects of language are difficult to reproduce in printed form, especially in ways that are easily recognisable in parts of the country distant from the areas exemplified. Too often, pupils simply end up 'spotting' non-standard forms and gain little sense of the vigour and expressiveness of regional variations – something that is given much greater emphasis with audio- or video-recordings or the 'live' resources provided by staffroom colleagues!

Reading and understanding

Many teachers will also want to read through the 'comprehension' text with their class and provide an introduction to the passage and the questions, although this should not be strictly necessary.

Pupils will need opportunities to study complete works of literature in their own right and, at the end of the key stage, to practise specific skills in preparation for the National Curriculum tests. The assumption has been made that writers and texts specified in the National Curriculum will be studied alongside the work contained here. Hence, an attempt has been made to look beyond the work of the prescribed writers – apart from Shakespeare – and represent simply the sort of range of reading that the National Curriculum requires.

Language, grammar and writing

The sections which focus on learning about language, word and text building are, again, intended to be worked through by teacher and pupils together. With some classes, little further explanation will be necessary and pupils will be able to work through the skills practice sections quite independently. In other cases, additional explanation may be required and teachers will want to reinforce learning by targeting the specific needs of individual pupils, using further materials of their own devising, possibly taking their cue from what is included here.

The skills practice exercises are intended to focus on particular points which are then practised – in the same way as a sports person spends hours practising individual skills – until they are handled with confidence. In the same way that the games-player's skills only have real significance within the context of the game, so the individual literacy/grammar skills serve no purpose if they cannot be integrated into each pupil's own writing and response to reading to enhance the quality of the work.

The intention behind the way material is presented in this book is that, once pupils have practised individual skills, discussion needs to focus on how these elements are brought together, discovering how different texts have different grammars. The relationship between choice of language, structure and meaning needs to be explored as pupils become increasingly sophisticated language-users themselves, leading on to consideration of issues related to genre and genre characteristics. Most teachers will want to integrate such discussions with development of the suggestions in the writing sections to suit their own pupils, giving a clear emphasis to the specific skills on which each individual pupil will need to concentrate.

Interaction essential

It is possible to work progressively through the book, and particularly teachers who do not have specialist subject expertise may find it advantageous to do so. Others may wish to use material more selectively, choosing specific units of work that address those skills their pupils need to acquire.

By its very nature, learning English is a process in which the schemes of work keep 'spiralling round', re-visiting the same skills, gradually broadening their base and strengthening them by using an ever-increasing range of materials and activities. This book is intended to be a useful 'tool of the trade', but like all other tools, will only be effective when deployed with the best skills of the craftsman – the teacher.

John Green

Unit 1: Basic essentials

In this unit you will:

- read the opening chapters of an unusual story;
- learn about the sentence, a structure fundamental to all written and spoken communication;
- learn about word stems and endings (suffixes);
- practise recognising different types of sentences and punctuating them correctly;
- practise building some new words by using suffixes.

Speaking and listening

- With a partner, think back to your earliest attempts at writing in your primary school, for example, diary writing, 'what I did on Saturday', 'special occasions', 'my holiday', 'our family pets'.

- What did you find hardest? Was it forming the letters, spelling, finding the right words, or using full stops and capital letters?

Understanding

Read this passage from the beginning of a book called *Flowers for Algernon* by Daniel Keyes. The central character is Charlie Gordon, an adult with learning difficulties, who is telling us about his experiences.

progris riport 1 martch 3

Dr Strauss says I shoud rite down what I think and remembir and evrey thing that happins to me from now on. I dont no why but he says its importint so they will see if they can use me. I hope they use me becaus Miss Kinnian says mabye they can
5 make me smart. I want to be smart. My name is Charlie Gordon I werk in Donners bakery where Mr Donner gives me 11 dollers a week and bred or cake if I want. I am 32 yeres old and next munth is my brithday. I tolld dr Strauss and perfesser Nemur I cant rite good but he says it dont matter he says I shud rite just
10 like I talk and like I rite compushishens in Miss Kinnians class at the beekmin collidge centre for retarted adults where I go to lern 3 times a week on my time off. Dr. Strauss says to rite a lot evrything I think and evrything that happins to me but I cant think anymor because I have nothing to rite so I will close for
15 today … yrs truly
Charlie Gordon.

progris riport 2 – martch 4

I had a test today. I think I faled it and I think mabye now they wont use me. What happind is I went to Prof Nemurs office on
20 my lunch time like they said and his secertery took me to a place that said psych dept on the door with a long hall and alot of littel rooms with onley a desk and chares. And a nice man was in one of the rooms and he had some wite cards with ink spilld all over them. He sed sit down Charlie and make
25 yourself cunfortible and rilax. He had a wite coat like a docter

continued …

but I dont think he was no docter because he dint tell me to opin my mouth and say ah. All he had was those wite cards. His name is Burt. I fergot his last name because I dont remembir so good.

30   I dint know what he was gonna do and I was holding on tite to the chair like sometimes when I go to a dentist onley Burt aint no dentist neither but he kept telling me to rilax and that gets me skared because it always means its gonna hert.

So Burt sed Charlie what do you see on this card. I saw the
35 spilld ink and I was very skared even tho I got my rabits foot in my pockit because when I was a kid I always faled tests in school and I spilld ink to.

I tolld Burt I saw ink spilld on a wite card. Burt said yes and he smild and that maid me feel good. He kept terning all the
40 cards and I tolld him somebody spilld ink on all of them red and black. I thot that was a easy test but when I got up to go Burt stoppd me and said now sit down Charlie we are not thru yet. Theres more we got to do with these cards. I dint understand about it but I remembir Dr Strauss said do anything the testor
45 telld me even if it dont make no sense because thats testing.

I dont remembir so good what Burt said but I remembir he wantid me to say what was in the ink. I dint see nothing in the ink but Burt sed there was picturs there. I couldnt see no picturs. I reely tryed to see. I holded the card up close and then
50 far away. Then I said if I had my eye glassis I coud probaly see better I usully only ware my eyeglassis in the movies or to watch TV but I sed maybe they will help me see the picturs in the ink. I put them on and I said now let me see the card agan I bet I find it now.

55   I tryed hard but I still coudnt find the picturs I only saw the ink. I tolld Burt mabey I need new glassis. He rote somthing down on a paper and I got skared of faling the test. So I tolld him it was a very nice pictur of ink with pritty points all around

the eges but he shaked his head so that wasnt it neither. I asked
60 him if other pepul saw things in the ink and he sed yes they
imagen picturs in the inkblot. He tolld me the ink on the card
was calld inkblot.

Burt is very nice and he talks slow like Miss Kinnian dose in
her class where I go to lern reeding for slow adults. He
65 explaned me it was a raw shok test. He sed pepul see things in
the ink. I said show me where. He dint show me he just kept
saying think imagen theres something on the card. I tolld him I
imaggen a inkblot. He shaked his head so that wasnt rite eather.

He said what does it remind you of pretend its something. I
70 closd my eyes for a long time to pretend and then I said I
pretend a bottel of ink spilld all over a wite card. And thats
when the point on his pencel broke and then we got up and
went out.

I dont think I passd the raw shok test.

Jot down answers to the following questions as they occur to
you. You need not write in sentences. Although at this stage in
the book you have not discussed any of the rules of spelling and
grammar, the questions assume you already know some of these.
This may mean you find it difficult to write comments in answer
to some questions, but it will help you to realise there are some
rules you do already know, although you may not have written
them out in an organised way.

1 What makes this piece of writing different from 'normal'
writing in a book? How difficult did you find it to read and
understand?

2 Make a list of the types of mistakes Charlie makes. For
example, there are obviously spelling mistakes, but what
patterns do you notice in the spelling mistakes? Does he have
trouble with particular sorts of words or parts of words? Which
of his mistakes are similar to the mistakes you used to make?

3 Despite the mistakes, we are still able to understand what Charlie is writing. Which rules of grammar, spelling and punctuation does he use to help us?

4 Now you have read and talked about the passage, what rules of grammar, spelling and punctuation do you think must be correctly used to make the meaning clear?

Learning about language: *sentences*

The sentence is fundamental to all written and spoken communication. **A sentence is a group of words that makes complete sense by itself.** When we speak or write groups of words that are not sentences, something else has to be added if we are to understand what we are being told. For example, if Charlie had begun his second report with 'I had a' we have to add more information, in this case 'test today', to understand the sentence.

Sentences may be long and complex or as short as one word. For example, 'Help!' or 'Wait!' may both make complete sense in the context in which they are used.

A sentence may be:

■ **a statement**
'Today's winner is Sunil.'

■ **a question**
'Who chose this tie?'

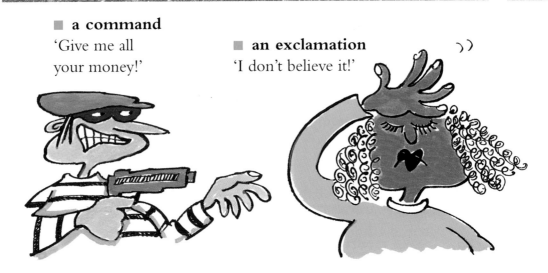

■ **a command**
'Give me all
your money!'

■ **an exclamation**
'I don't believe it!'

Sentences usually have a **subject** – who or what the rest of the sentence (often called the predicate) is about.

For example: In the sentence 'I am writing a report'
'I' is the subject – who the sentence is about;
'am writing a report' is the predicate – what the subject is doing.

In the sentence 'Swallows fly south in winter'
'Swallows' is the subject – who the sentence is about; 'fly south in winter' is the predicate – what the subject is doing.

Sentences also often have an **object** – who or what has been affected by the action of the verb.

For example: In the sentence 'His secretary took me to another room', 'me' is the object – who or what was affected by the action 'took'.

In the sentence 'I knocked over a bottle of ink'
'a bottle of ink' is the object – who or what was affected by the action 'knocked over'.

Skills practice: *recognising sentences*

Check the examples given on pages 8 and 9 and then work your way through the following exercises.

Remember the rule:

- A sentence is a group of words that makes complete sense by itself.

Exercise A

Write down whether each group of words is a statement, a question or not a sentence at all. *(Hint: look for clues from the punctuation.)*

  1 I look forward to the holidays.

  2 My cat chases all the dogs in our street.

  3 To the dustbins, you can

  4 Where have you put my books?

  5 What size do you need?

  6 If only there

  7 I feel exhausted.

  8 Have you been running?

  9 I'm busy doing my homework.

10 Why don't you like Mondays?

Exercise B

Write down whether each of these sentences is a command, exclamation, statement or question.

  1 I am not going to school today.

  2 What on earth is that?

  3 Look out!

  4 Why should I be punished?

  5 Good grief!

  6 My English teacher really annoys me.

  7 Beware of the bull!

  8 May I have some more?

  9 Take cover!

10 Amazing!

Exercise C

Now do it yourself! Make up two more examples of each – statements, questions, commands and exclamations.

Exercise D

Copy out these sentences and underline or highlight the subject in one colour and the object in another. Not every sentence has an object.

1 I persuaded him to leave.
2 Our class is preparing a nativity play for Christmas.
3 Danny kicked the ball into touch.
4 Liz met her grandparents at the station.
5 An old exercise book lay in the middle of the puddle.
6 The doctor wrote out a prescription.
7 Laurie saw him in the street only yesterday.
8 Richard and Tom were reading quietly.
9 Our neighbour's dog really frightened me.
10 Homework must be handed in promptly.

Word building: *stems and suffixes*

Words are made up of different parts. The central or essential part of a word is called the **stem** or **root**. The stem sometimes stands alone but may also, as its name suggests, be the part of the word from which other words can grow.

Often an ending is added to the stem of a word to change its grammatical form or function. This ending is called a **suffix**.

For example, Charlie works in a **bakery**. The stem of this word is **bake**; a simple suffix (-r) creates a word for his boss, Mr Donner, who is a bake**r**; another suffix (-ry) creates a word for the place where he works, a bake**ry**.

Another suffix that appears quite often in the passage is -ed (although sometimes Charlie misspells this as -d). This suffix is used to indicate that the action being described took place in the past. For example, Charlie writes about how he thinks he 'faled' (failed) the test and tells us what 'happind' (happened). These two words are built up from their stems – 'fail' and 'happen' – with the addition of a suffix. In later chapters, we shall look at the meaning and function of different suffixes in more detail.

Skills practice: *word stems and suffixes*

Complete this table by dividing the words into a stem and suffix. Think of another suffix that could be added to the stem to create a new word. The first row has been completed as an example.

Word	Stem	Suffix	New word
failed	fail	–ed	failure
successor			
spilled			
comfortable			
smiled			
attractive			
commandment			
cloudless			

Text building: *sentence markers*

The words in a sentence must be in an order that makes sense. Sentences are divided off from each other by sentence markers. The first word of a sentence is given a capital letter and a full stop is put after the last word. Imagine how much more difficult it would have been to understand the beginning of Charlie's second report if he had left out the punctuation: 'I had a test today i think I faled it and I think maybe now they wont use me what happind …'.

Two other sentence markers are needed when a sentence is not a statement. If it is a question, it has a question mark (?) at the end; if it is a command or an exclamation it has an exclamation mark (!).

Skills practice: *sentence markers*

Remember the rules (check the examples on pages 8 and 9):

- the first word of a sentence is given a capital letter;
- a full stop is placed after the last word if the sentence is a statement;
- a question mark (?) is placed after the last word if the sentence is a question;
- an exclamation mark (!) is placed after the last word if the sentence is an exclamation.

Exercise A

Add capital letters and full stops to the following:

1 he has been in the army for two years
2 she has always been left-handed
3 i have read the instructions
4 they helped us to push the car
5 after three hours we arrived at the campsite
6 yesterday was really enjoyable
7 this train will arrive in approximately ten minutes
8 i prefer English to history
9 the shops will be crowded
10 she explained how to use the parachute

Exercise B

Add sentence markers (punctuation) to the following:

1 where have all the flowers gone
2 sit down quietly
3 he should be here by now
4 what a crazy scheme
5 will you come round on Saturday
6 she says they are going to visit her family
7 close that window
8 mind your backs
9 my mother has to work at weekends
10 can you understand all this

Exercise C

This passage is taken from a later stage in the book when Charlie's writing skills have much improved. Copy out this extract, adding sentence markers to make it even easier to understand.

> We got out of the car and walked over to one of the cottages inside the walls were white tiles and the building had a disinfectant smell to it the first floor lobby opened up to a recreation room filled with some seventy boys sitting around waiting for the lunch bell to be sounded what caught my eye immediately was one of the bigger boys on a chair in the corner comforting one of the other boys in his arms they all turned to look at me as we entered and some of the bolder ones came over and stared at me.
>
> (Adapted from *Flowers for Algernon* by Daniel Keyes)

ICT Extra!

Using spelling and grammar checkers
Type the first 15 lines from *Flowers for Algernon* (page 5) into your computer. Run the text through your computer's spellcheck (and grammar check if it has one). List the corrections the check highlights. Look for any similarities in the mistakes that you have made and try to divide them into groups. Keep this list for reference as you learn more about spelling and punctuation rules in future units.

Writing

Imagine you, like Charlie, are going to report on a special event or 'big occasion' in your life. It could be something like a birthday, a family wedding or the first day at a new school.

Write three short diary entries:

- one about the day before, dealing with the excitement, anticipation, 'nerves', etc;

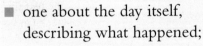
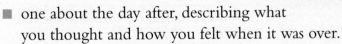

- one about the day itself, describing what happened;

- one about the day after, describing what you thought and how you felt when it was over.

As well as making your reports as interesting as possible, concentrate on correctly using the punctuation skills you have practised in this unit.

Unit 2: Gathering information

In this unit you will:

- read an advertisement for information;
- learn about nouns;
- learn about using suffixes to make nouns;
- practise building nouns and using the comma in lists.

Speaking and listening

- Look at the catalogue page below and find out which is the cheapest bicycle.

- With a partner, compile a list of four occasions when you might consult a list – an index or a catalogue, for example.

- What are such 'lists' useful for? How do they 'work'?

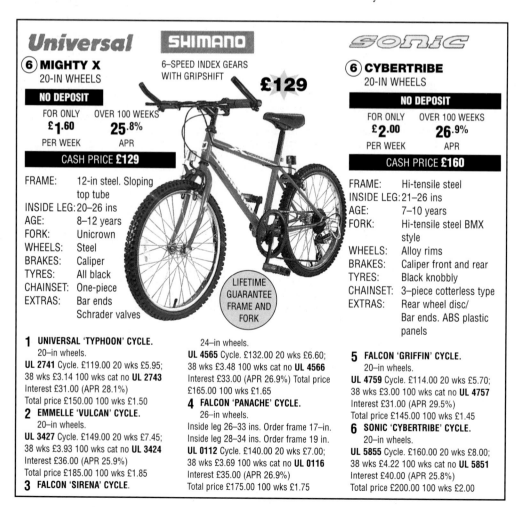

Universal

6 MIGHTY X
20-IN WHEELS

NO DEPOSIT

FOR ONLY £1.60 PER WEEK

OVER 100 WEEKS 25.8% APR

CASH PRICE £129

FRAME: 12-in steel. Sloping top tube
INSIDE LEG: 20–26 ins
AGE: 8–12 years
FORK: Unicrown
WHEELS: Steel
BRAKES: Caliper
TYRES: All black
CHAINSET: One-piece
EXTRAS: Bar ends
             Schrader valves

SHIMANO

6–SPEED INDEX GEARS WITH GRIPSHIFT

£129

LIFETIME GUARANTEE FRAME AND FORK

SONIC

6 CYBERTRIBE
20-IN WHEELS

NO DEPOSIT

FOR ONLY £2.00 PER WEEK

OVER 100 WEEKS 26.9% APR

CASH PRICE £160

FRAME: Hi-tensile steel
INSIDE LEG: 21–26 ins
AGE: 7–10 years
FORK: Hi-tensile steel BMX style
WHEELS: Alloy rims
BRAKES: Caliper front and rear
TYRES: Black knobbly
CHAINSET: 3–piece cotterless type
EXTRAS: Rear wheel disc/ Bar ends. ABS plastic panels

1 UNIVERSAL 'TYPHOON' CYCLE.
20–in wheels.
UL 2741 Cycle. £119.00 20 wks £5.95; 38 wks £3.14 100 wks cat no **UL 2743**
Interest £31.00 (APR 28.1%)
Total price £150.00 100 wks £1.50
2 EMMELLE 'VULCAN' CYCLE.
20–in wheels.
UL 3427 Cycle. £149.00 20 wks £7.45; 38 wks £3.93 100 wks cat no **UL 3424**
Interest £36.00 (APR 25.9%)
Total price £185.00 100 wks £1.85
3 FALCON 'SIRENA' CYCLE.

24–in wheels.
UL 4565 Cycle. £132.00 20 wks £6.60; 38 wks £3.48 100 wks cat no **UL 4566**
Interest £33.00 (APR 26.9%) Total price £165.00 100 wks £1.65
4 FALCON 'PANACHE' CYCLE.
26–in wheels.
Inside leg 26–33 ins. Order frame 17–in. Inside leg 28–34 ins. Order frame 19 in.
UL 0112 Cycle. £140.00 20 wks £7.00; 38 wks £3.69 100 wks cat no **UL 0116**
Interest £35.00 (APR 26.9%)
Total price £175.00 100 wks £1.75

5 FALCON 'GRIFFIN' CYCLE.
20–in wheels.
UL 4759 Cycle. £114.00 20 wks £5.70; 38 wks £3.00 100 wks cat no **UL 4757**
Interest £31.00 (APR 29.5%)
Total price £145.00 100 wks £1.45
6 SONIC 'CYBERTRIBE' CYCLE.
20–in wheels.
UL 5855 Cycle. £160.00 20 wks £8.00; 38 wks £4.22 100 wks cat no **UL 5851**
Interest £40.00 (APR 25.8%)
Total price £200.00 100 wks £2.00

Understanding

Most of us read to find out information, whether we are reading a train timetable or an instruction manual. These questions will test your understanding of basic facts. You need to focus on specific details to show you have read the text carefully and understand the information it is giving.

Read this advertisement announcing an auction sale and answer the questions below and on page 18:

DEE ATKINSON & HARRISON
THE EXCHANGE SALEROOM, DRIFFIELD, EAST YORKSHIRE
FRIDAY 26th SEPTEMBER AT 10.00 a.m.

ANTIQUE AND LATER FURNITURE, CERAMICS
Collectors items, Miscellaneous, Silver, Silverplate and Jewellery including a substantial Private Collection of Oils and Watercolours.
A fine 17th Century Oyster veneered chest, inlaid Victorian walnut Credenza, oak Monk's bench, inlaid Edwardian mahogany display cabinet, Victorian mahogany secretaire bookcase, small Victorian marquetry circular table, Victorian and Georgian mahogany chests of drawers, set of four Victorian mahogany dining chairs, antique mahogany chest on chest. Victorian button back chairs, octagonal walnut veneered 1930's display cabinet, Victorian mahogany mirror back sideboard, Camphor wood travelling box, Victorian corner what-not, 19th Century swing dressing table mirrors, antique mahogany and inlaid lowboy, 19th Century French ormolu and parquetry cabinet, etc.
CERAMICS: Beswick, Royal Doulton, Noritake, Clarice Cliff, Sylvac, Royal Crown Derby, Royal Winton, Victorian and later part tea and coffee sets, Staffordshire figures, Crown Derby, 2 Fairings etc.
GLASS: Six old chemists bottles, pair of 19th Century clear glass lustres, decanters, Cranberry jug and two small tumblers together with a selection of Victorian and later drinking glasses etc.
MISCELLANEOUS: Cased birds, brass and copper, fountain pens, fine ivory handled walking stick, 19th Century rocking horse, vintage bride's veil, Hummell doll, books, clocks, stereoscope, rugs including two Disney rugs, Victorian tea caddy etc.
SILVER, SILVER PLATE & JEWELLERY: A selection of Georgian, Victorian and later silver and silver plate including a fine Viners Canteen of silver cutlery 12 place settings, pair of Georgian silver basting and serving spoons, Edwardian silver Rose Bowl, Georgian silver caster, Edwardian 3 piece silver tea set,

cased set of Victorian EPNS fish knives and forks, large EPNS salver, a good selection of Victorian and later jewellery including gold and silver pocket watches, Masonic jewels, Jensen silver bracelet, gold Albert and gold bracelets, rings, mourning brooch, plated Chatelaine, etc.
FROM A SUBSTANTIAL PRIVATE COLLECTION, OILS AND WATER COLOURS:
To include works by W. D. Penny, Fred Elwell, Mary Elwell, Walter Goodin, John Bromley, W. Rogers, Ralph Stubbs, Harry Williams, Calvert R. Jones, Ludwig Offermans, E. K. Redmore, William Settle, Frank H. Mason, Claud Hayes, Edwin Hayes, Ralph Dodd, D. Farquharson, etc.

VIEWING
Wednesday,
24th September,
10 a.m. – 7 p.m. &
Thursday,
25th September,
10 a.m. – 4 p.m.
Limited viewing on
morning of sale.
Catalogues £4.50
including p & p.

E-Mail address: daandh@globalnet.co.uk
INTERNET:
http://www.thesaurus.co.uk/deeatkinson&harrison/
THESAURUS FAX BACK SERVICE
Instant catalogue available by dialling 0891 616988 from your touch-tone fax machine, when answered press 5181 for a summary of the selections available. Calls are charged at 38p per minute cheap rate – 49p at other times.
THE EXCHANGE, DRIFFIELD,
EAST YORKSHIRE
(01377) 253151

---

1 What is the name of the company organising the sale?

2 When and where will the sale take place?

3 When may the items for sale be viewed?

4 How else can advance information be obtained about the items for sale?

5 How much does a catalogue cost?

6 From what period does most of the furniture date?

7 Name three makes of china included in the ceramics sale.

8 If you were a fan of Disney films, what might you be interested in bidding for?

9 If you needed a set of knives and forks, what might you be interested in bidding for?

10 Which item do you think is shown in the photograph?

Learning about language: *nouns*

The auction advertisement contains the names of the objects that are for sale. Words that name things are called **nouns**.

A noun is a naming word.

Nouns may be the name of a person, a thing, a place or an idea.

For example:

■ **a person**

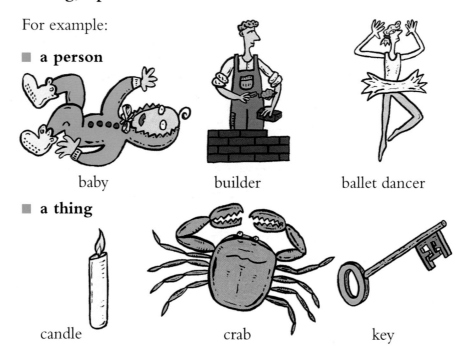

baby   builder   ballet dancer

■ **a thing**

candle   crab   key

■ **a place**

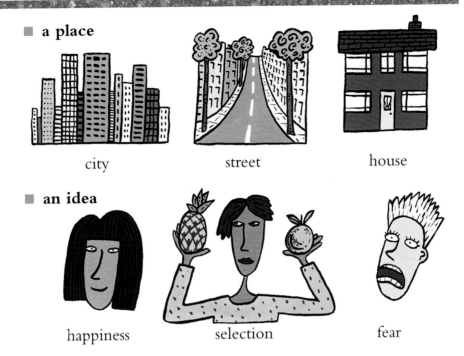

city   street   house

■ **an idea**

happiness   selection   fear

Skills practice: *recognising nouns*

Remember the rule:

■ A noun is a naming word. It can be a person, a thing, a place or an idea.

Exercise A

Check the examples on pages 18 and 19, then copy out these sentences, underlining the nouns in each.

   1 The boy was walking his dog through the park.

   2 The girl in the blue dress was pulling faces at the teacher.

   3 Do you think scientists will ever manage to clone dinosaurs?

   4 The auctioneer banged his gavel on the desk.

   5 That antique chair is worth a lot of money.

   6 What shall we do with the lost dog?

   7 Is there pizza for tea?

   8 Mum is going to buy a new car.

   9 Shut that door immediately!

   10 Please let me have another biscuit.

Exercise B

Copy out these sentences and fill the gaps with nouns. (You may choose nouns that make the meaning amusing or unexpected.)

1 Shall I take my .... to .... today?

2 The baby threw its .... out of the ....

3 The .... was next to the ....

4 Will you put that .... down!

5 Why do I have to copy out this .... ?

6 My .... would rather play .... than ....

7 The .... is jumping over the ....

8 Where have I left my .... ?

9 Please don't feed the ....

10 My .... lies over the ....

Word building: *noun suffixes*

Look back at the examples of nouns on pages 18 and 19 and check how many are made up of a **stem** plus a **suffix**. For example, build/-**er**, select/-**ion**. Suffixes are often added to a word stem to create nouns that are the names of people or places.

Now concentrate on people who do things. The commonest suffixes, meaning 'the person who does' or 'the person who is connected with', are –or, –er and –ar.

For example: sail-or   sing-er   begg-ar★

(★ *Note the doubling of the 'g'*).

Two other suffixes for 'people who do certain things' are –ist and –ian.

For example: motor-ist   music-ian   electric-ian

Skills practice: *creating nouns*

Exercise A

Add the suffixes –or, –er or –ar – whichever is appropriate – to the following word stems to make nouns. The first one has been done for you as an example.

Stem	Noun formed with –or/–er/–ar
select	*selector*
inform	
visit	
murder	
jump	
call	
collect	
sleep	
exhibit	
school*	

(* Watch out! This is a slightly irregular form!)

Exercise B

Add the suffixes –ist or –ian – whichever is appropriate – to the following word stems to make nouns. The first one has been done for you as an example.

Stem	Noun formed with –ist/–ian
tour	*tourist*
art	
terror	
politics*	
mathematics*	
cartoon	
psychiatry*	
piano*	
botany*	
canoe	

(* Note: the last letter of the stem is often dropped or changed.)

Text building: *lists*

You will notice that the items listed for sale in the auction advertisement on page 17 are separated from each other by a **comma** (,). Just as sentence markers are used to make understanding easier by separating sentences, so the comma is used in lists to ensure that there is no confusion between the items.

A comma is used to separate items in a list. However, no comma is needed before the final item in the list if a linking word such as 'and' is used.

For example: I had egg, sausage, bacon, beans **and** toast for breakfast.

Skills practice: *commas*

Exercise A
Add commas in the following lists:

1   A high quality blend of natural ingredients including malt vinegar tomatoes molasses spirit vinegar dates sugar salt raisins cornflour rye flour tamarind spices soy sauce mustard onion extract.
(A well known brand of brown sauce!)

2   This pack contains two door panels two side panels one backing sheet one base six shelves 12 wooden dowling plugs 24 shelf brackets and 4 hinge packs.
(Do-it-yourself bookcase pack)

3   When staying in London be sure to visit St Paul's Cathedral Westminster Abbey the Houses of Parliament Whitehall and Downing Street Buckingham Palace Oxford Street for shopping Trafalgar Square to feed
the pigeons the National Gallery the National Portrait Gallery and the Tower of London. (Tourist Guide to London)

Exercise B
Add sentence markers and commas where necessary in the following:
(Hint: some sentence breaks are indicated for you by / /.)

I walked along the street and turned into the first shop// I needed bread milk sugar// inside the shop I immediately recognised my friends Martin Anil

Michael and the twins it took me some time to find what I needed and by the time I arrived at the checkout I had added chicken legs chips tomato sauce marmalade and croissants to my original list the woman in front of me in the queue seemed to know the checkout operator and she spent ages telling them about her operation her grandchildren her cats and the cost of living// eventually she left and it was my turn// I paid collected my receipt packed my bags and set off for home.

Writing

Your parents have told you to 'clear the junk out of your room'! You decide to have a 'grand sale' for your friends.

■ Prepare a poster, listing and describing the items available, as well as giving other relevant information (where and when the sale is to be held, for example).

■ Concentrate on giving the poster impact, for example, by highlighting interesting and attractive items so that people will be keen to come. Make sure any lists of items are clearly set out and properly punctuated.

(Hint: look back at the auction advertisement at the beginning of this unit. Think about how much – or how little – impact it made on you, and then try to produce something more eye-catching and informative.)

 ICT Extra!

Desktop publishing
You could use desktop publishing facilities to complete this task, taking advantage of a range of type-faces and font sizes, borders and 'bullet points'. If you have really advanced facilities you could even scan in small photographs of some objects.

Unit 3: What happened?

In this unit you will:

- read an extract from a novel about a young boy called Joby;
- learn about verbs;
- learn about using suffixes to make verbs;
- practise finding lively and interesting verbs to brighten up your writing.

Speaking and listening

- Describe to a partner something that happened to you before you arrived at school this morning.

- Concentrate on saying precisely what happened and make sure everything is included in the right order.

Understanding

In the previous units you were tested on your understanding of the information you were given. Here the focus is still on selecting specific details to make sure you have read the text carefully, but this time you need to understand the story line.

Read the extract on the following pages from *Joby* by Stan Barstow and then answer the questions.

The story is set in a northern town in 1939, just before the beginning of the Second World War. Two 12-year-old boys, Joby and Gus, go shoplifting.

He put two pennies into Gus's hand and Gus opened the door, setting a bell jangling. The inside of the shop was quiet and cool. There were jars of jam and lemon cheese, and cans of all kinds of things piled high on the shelves against the wall; boxes of sweets
5 and custard powders on the L-shaped counter and an open sack of potatoes and another of sugar on the floor. They listened for someone coming but there was no sound from anywhere.

When Gus dipped his hand into a box of toffees it was like a signal to Joby. He followed suit while Gus, cool as you please,
10 stretched himself right over the width of the counter to reach the cigarettes. At the back of Joby's mind as he stuffed handfuls of sweets into his pockets was the thought that the shopkeeper was a very long time in coming.

And just then the voice, like a kick to the heart, said,
15   'And what d'you think you're doing?'

They sprang round, their bodies stiffening into motionless attitudes of flight as they saw that the man was on their side of the counter, between them and the door. Shock robbed them of their voices. They gaped at him, saying nothing. The
20 shopkeeper, a thin, elderly man in a khaki smock, reached out and slid the bolt on the door, cutting off all hope of escape.

'I asked you what you thought you were doing.'

His voice was stiff and cold as iron. Joby, weak with shock and fright, thought he had never heard a voice like it, nor seen a face
25 so hard and ungiving as this man's. Oh! but he had dreaded this from the first. He had known it must happen some time. If only they could go back ten minutes and be playing with the ball in the street and no thought of the shop in their heads!

Gus managed to speak.
30   'We wanted some chewing gum, please,' he said, as though he didn't understand the man.

continued …

'Yes, that's right,' Joby heard himself babbling. 'Just some chewing gum. He's got the money for it.' He gestured towards Gus who opened his hand and showed the two pennies in

35 his palm.

'Chewing gum, eh? Well, you won't find any in that box o' toffees, not under the counter, either!'

He squared his thin shoulders inside the khaki smock. His bushy grey eyebrows frothed over the rims of his spectacles

40 and his eyes were bright and hard as he looked at them. He waved his hand towards the rear premises.

'You'd better go through there wi' me. Go on, now, let's be having you!'

Now answer these questions in note form:

1 Who was holding the money as the boys entered the shop?

2 What was the signal for Joby to start stealing?

3 What two things did Gus steal?

4 Why did the boys not notice the shopkeeper?

5 How did the shopkeeper stop the boys running away?

6 What had the boys been doing ten minutes before?

7 What kind of voice did the shopkeeper have?

8 What did the boys say they wanted to buy?

9 What was the shopkeeper wearing?

10 Where did he take the boys?

Learning about language: *verbs*

In the passage, the main focus of attention is on what the boys do. Words that indicate an action are called **verbs**.

A verb is a doing or action word.

For example:

- The lion is roaring.

- I am eating spaghetti.

- This man is pointing to his right.

- A **verb** explains the **action** between people or things.

  For example:
  'He put two pennies into Gus's hand.'

- Or **what is happening**. For example:
  'They listened for someone coming.'

Skills practice: *recognising verbs*

Exercise A

Copy out these sentences and underline or highlight the verbs.

1 I walk to school, but Karen goes on the bus.
2 My cat chases all the dogs in our street.
3 My English teacher really annoys me.
4 Sit down quietly.
5 People crowded into the shop as soon as the sale started.
6 The team ran out on the pitch.
7 Read the instructions carefully.
8 I saw her at the concert last week.
9 My mother works most evenings.
10 Wood always floats.

Exercise B

Copy out these sentences and fill the gaps with suitable verbs. (You may choose verbs that make the meaning amusing or unexpected.)

1 She .... how the parachute worked.

2 I .... my dog for a walk every evening.

3 Water .... at 0°C.

4 The workman .... and ....

5 Please .... the building immediately.

6 I .... the piano every day.

7 Why .... a coat this morning? .... your umbrella instead!

8 Her behaviour really .... me.

9 Every time he .... his mouth, he .... something stupid.

10 The travel agency .... them to return home at once.

Word building: *verb suffixes*

You have practised adding **suffixes** to a word **stem** to create nouns. Suffixes may also be used to create **verbs**. These often mean 'to make ...' (whatever the stem might be).

For example:

- length + –en gives lengthen, meaning 'to make something longer'
- soft + –en gives soften, meaning 'to make something softer'
- false + –ify gives falsify (note the –e is dropped), meaning 'to make something untrue or false'
- simple + –ify gives simplify (again, the –e is dropped), meaning 'to make something simpler'.

Skills practice

Exercise A

Add the suffix –en to the following words to create verbs. The first one has been done for you. Make sure you know what the new verbs mean.

Stem	Verb
strength	strengthen
hard	
sharp	
wide*	
tight	
rough	
thick	
less	
fat*	

(* *Take care with the spelling of the verb here!*)

Exercise B

Creating verbs by adding the suffix –ify is more complicated than adding -en because the last letter (and sometimes more than one) of the stem often has to be removed first.

For example: with **beauty** you must remove the **–y** before you add **–ify** to make **beaut–ify**.

The words where you need to make changes like this are marked * in the table below.

Now add the suffix –ify to the following words to create verbs. The first one has been done for you. Remember to make sure you know what the new verbs mean.

Stem	Verb
solid	solidify
just	
null	
pure*	
identity*	
liquid*	
simple	
terror*	
mystery*	

Text building: *choosing verbs*

Look again at this paragraph from the passage about Joby and Gus.

> They *sprang* round, their bodies *stiffening* into motionless attitudes of flight as they saw that the man was on their side of the counter, between them and the door. Shock *robbed* them of their voices. They *gaped* at him, saying nothing. The shopkeeper, a thin, elderly man in a khaki smock, reached out and *slid* the bolt on the door, cutting off all hope of escape.

Some of the verbs have been emphasised to show you that they add greater interest and energy to the way the boys' actions are described. For example, 'They turned round' would hardly suggest the speed with which the boys reacted. Why is 'They gaped at him' more effective than 'They looked at him'?

Think how much more vividly you would describe someone's progress along the street if, instead of using 'walking', you said they were 'stumbling', 'bustling', 'staggering' or 'wandering'. All these words bring a different picture of your character's movements into the mind's eye.

 ICT Extra!

Using a computer's thesaurus
Use the thesaurus within your computer to find four verbs to describe 'going up'. Is there a difference in meaning between these verbs? Write four sentences using each of these verbs correctly.

Skills practice

Exercise A

'Said' can be a very boring word when over-used! Look at these words:

whispered	stammered	hissed	snarled
shrieked	yelled	commanded	demanded
bawled	growled	shouted	implored
uttered	groaned	moaned	affirmed
pronounced	announced	dictated	preached
lectured	ranted	recited	muttered
screamed	drawled	gushed	droned
murmured	purred	crooned	sighed
squeaked	croaked		

Can you add any words of your own which can be used instead? Look up the meaning of any words you are not sure of and then complete the following sentences.

1 'Get out of this room,' she ………

2 'I'm frightened,' he ………

3 'Not you again!' she ………

4 'Please, please, consider it,' he ………

5 'She's a sweet little dog,' she ………

6 'You'll do as you're told,' he ………

7 'Name and address,' he ………

8 'Don't say you've forgotten it,' she ………

9 'It may be true,' he ………

10 'Is it really too late?' she ………

Exercise B

Write down four verbs to add to 'stumbling', 'bustling', 'staggering' and 'wandering' to describe ways of 'walking'.

Exercise C

Write down four verbs to describe ways of eating.

Exercise D

Replace the highlighted verbs in the passage that follows (page 32) with another verb of similar meaning that conveys a more vivid picture. Compare your suggestions with your partner and come up with a 'best' version, perhaps even improving on Conan Doyle's original!

(Hint: choose some of these verbs – bounded; worry; hunting; paralysed; spring.)

continued …

With long bounds the huge black creature *was moving* down the track, following hard upon the footsteps of our friend. So *surprised* were we by the apparition that we *let* him pass before we had recovered our nerve. Then Holmes and I fired together, and the creature gave a hideous howl. It did not pause, however, but *carried* onward. Far away on the path we saw Sir Henry looking back, his face white in the moonlight, his hands raised in horror at the frightful thing that was *chasing* him. In front of us as we *ran* up the track we heard scream after scream from Sir Henry, and the deep roar of

 the hound. I was in time to see the beast *jump* upon its victim, *push* him to the ground, and *sniff* at his throat. But the next instant Holmes had *fired* five barrels of his revolver into the creature's flank.

(Adapted from Chapter 14 of *The Hound of the Baskervilles* by A. Conan Doyle)

Writing

- Return to the Speaking and listening exercise at the start of this unit. It said:

  'Describe to a partner something that happened to you before you arrived at school this morning.'

- Now write a paragraph dealing with the incident you chose. This time make your account as lively and interesting as you possibly can by choosing verbs that will make your writing really dramatic.

Unit 4: Getting the picture

In this unit you will:

- read an extract from a travel book;
- learn about adjectives;
- learn about using suffixes to make adjectives;
- practise using adjectives to make your writing more vivid and interesting.

Speaking and listening

- With a partner, write down all the words that could be used to describe your bedroom or classroom. Choose another room you know well if you prefer.

(Hint: think about the five senses – sight, smell, taste, touch, hearing – and ask yourself how does the room look, what does it smell like, what can you hear? etc.)

- Now each of you write a paragraph describing the room, choosing your words carefully so that your description also conveys, as effectively as possible, how you feel about the room.

Understanding

In the previous unit, you looked at ways to make your own
writing livelier, by choosing verbs that give a vivid picture of the
action they describe.

Writers also choose words carefully to reveal the thoughts,
feelings and moods of their characters, sometimes, as in this
extract, by describing a scene or place. The questions that follow
this passage, from Paul Theroux's *The Kingdom by the Sea,* will test
whether you can make deductions or draw inferences from the
words the writer uses to describe things. You must refer to the
evidence from the text on which you base your comments.

*Paul Theroux set out to travel round the coast to find out what Britain
and the British are really like. This extract from Chapter 7 describes
Polperro in Cornwall.*

Polperro was a village of
whitewashed cottages
tumbled together in a
rocky ravine on the sea.

5 The streets were as
narrow as alleys and
few of them could take
motor vehicles. I saw a
full-sized bus try to make it down one street – hopeless.

10 At best, one small car could inch down a street knocking the
petals off geraniums in the windowboxes on either side. When
two cars met head-on there was usually an argument over who
was to reverse to let the other pass.

The loathing for tourists and outsiders in Cornwall was

15 undisguised. I had a feeling that it was the tourists who had
made the Cornish nationalistic, for no one adopted a funny native
costume quicker or talked more intimidatingly of local tradition
than the local person under siege by tourists. Polperro was a

pretty funnel but with the narrowest neck, so there was nowhere
20 to go but the tiny harbour. It was true that the Cornish derived
most of their income from tourists; but there was no contradiction
in the way they both welcomed and disliked us at the same time.
Natives always had very sound reasons for disliking outsiders; the
Cornish fishermen had nothing whatsoever to do with tourists,
25 but the other Cornish were farming people and treated tourists
like livestock – feeding them, fencing them in, and getting them to
move to new pastures. We were cumbersome burdens, a great
headache most of the time, but at the end of the day there was
some profit in us.

1 Explain what you think the writer feels about Polperro. You
should comment on:
■ whether he makes the village seem attractive or unpleasant;
■ which words in his description give you this impression.

2 What impression does the writer give of the attitude of
Polperro residents towards tourists and outsiders? You should
comment on:
■ the way visitors are treated by the locals;
■ the words the writer uses to describe the treatment
of visitors.

ICT Extra!

Finding a website
Find the website for Polperro and print it off. Compare the way Polperro is
presented on the website with the impressions given in the extract from
The Kingdom by the Sea. You should comment on:
■ the purpose of the website;
■ the use of pictures and the choice of information given.

Learning about language: *adjectives*

The description of Polperro contains a number of words that
describe various aspects of the place. Words that describe things
are called **adjectives**.

An adjective is a describing word that adds to the meaning of a noun by answering such questions as 'which?', 'how many?', 'what kind?'.

For example:

- 'a village of *whitewashed* cottages'
- 'a *rocky* ravine'
- 'a *full-sized* bus'.

Skills practice: *recognising adjectives*

Exercise A
Copy out these sentences and underline or highlight the adjective(s) in each.

1 The small boy was walking his scruffy dog through the park.

2 The pretty girl in the blue dress was laughing at the teacher.

3 I drove off in my shiny new car.

4 The sun beat down from a cloudless sky.

5 The angry wasp buzzed around her head.

6 Emma always liked bright, colourful clothes.

7 We had an enjoyable afternoon in town.

8 The scrapyard was full of dirty old wagons and trucks.

9 The cheerful smiles of the children suggested that school had finished.

10 The busy streets of south London bring back happy memories of my childhood.

Exercise B
Copy out these sentences and fill the gaps with suitable adjectives. (You may choose adjectives that make the meaning amusing or unexpected.)

1 The .... toddler threw her .... toy out of the buggy.

2 Will you put that .... book down!

3 My .... bike lay half-submerged in the .... pond.

4 Where shall I put this .... painting?

5 The .... crowd invaded the pitch.

6 The .... streets made it difficult for the bus to turn safely.

7 I stared at the .... dog in surprise.

8 The .... fox jumped over the .... fence.

9 Shall I put this .... flag in here?

10 The teenager put his .... rucksack on the .... table.

Word building: *adjective suffixes*

In the same way that nouns and verbs can be formed from a word stem plus a suffix, so can adjectives. Two common suffixes for making adjectives are –y and –ly.

For example: sand + –y gives sandy

grease + –y gives greasy (note the final 'e' is dropped)

month + –ly gives monthly

friend + –ly gives friendly

Skills practice

Exercise A

Add the suffix –y to the words in the table to create adjectives. The first one has been done for you.

Stem	Adjective
cloud	cloudy
wind	
oil	
mist	
silver	
rust	
salt	

Exercise B

Add the suffix –ly to the words in the table to create adjectives. The first one has been done for you as an example.

Stem	Adjective
ghost	ghostly
man	
elder	
hour	
earth	
mother	
day*	
week	

(* Note: take care over the spelling of the adjective you create with this word!)

Text building: *choosing adjectives*

Using vivid adjectives can add vigour and interest to writing in the same way as well chosen verbs can. Think how much more interesting 'The cat sat on the mat' might have been if only someone had used a few extra words to describe the cat and the mat.

Look at this picture of a monster and list four adjectives that might describe its:

- arms
- claws
- teeth
- tongue
- cheeks.

Skills practice: *choosing adjectives*

Exercise A

This is a rather boring piece of writing about Claire and the monster. Rewrite it, making the story more interesting by filling in the gaps with suitable adjectives you have listed.

Clare had walked a little way into the ...., ... wood, when she heard a .... noise. To her horror, a .... and .... creature stood in her way. It was tall and its ...., ... arms ended in .... claws. Behind its .... tongue were rows of ...., ... teeth.

'Go away you .... thing!' squealed Clare. The monster howled and two .... tears trickled down its .... cheeks.

Exercise B

Rewrite this simple description of a town to make it more colourful. You can add details which reflect life in a busy town. Above all, try to choose verbs and adjectives that bring the scene alive in your mind's eye and give some idea of your feelings about the place.

> The town had a canal running along past the railway station. There were a lot of warehouses nearby, but across the road some new office blocks. People were coming out of the car park, and then walking along the streets and looking into shop windows.

Writing

Return to the description of the room you drafted with your partner at the start of this unit. In the light of what you have now learned, rewrite it as a vivid and lively description of a familiar place.

Unit 5: Creating an impression

In this unit you will:

- read an advertisement and consider its effect;
- learn more about nouns;
- learn more about using suffixes to make nouns;
- practise building nouns and using the apostrophe to show ownership.

Speaking and listening

- With a partner, list some revolting objects everyone dislikes. For example, smelly socks, grubby tea towels, fish fingers full of bones and skin.

- Discuss and note down five ways you could give these things a new, more positive image.
- Save your notes for the end of this unit, when you will try to do just that.

Understanding

Many writers, especially copywriters for advertisers, choose words carefully to have a persuasive effect on the reader. Advertisements may also make use of pictures, colour and other aspects of layout, as well as thoughtfully chosen language to create an attractive 'image'.

'Franki' is an imaginary range of toiletries created as a project by a Year 11 Business Studies class. Here is one of the advertisements intended to introduce the product to young teenagers. Read it through and answer the questions that follow.

1 What is the first thing you notice about this advertisement?

2 What effects are achieved by the choice of colours that are used?

3 A lot of adjectives, such as 'fresh' and 'cool' are used in this advertisement. Write down another five adjectives and explain the impression they are intended to create.

4 What effect is intended by the choice of phrases like 'organic herbs', 'mountain spring water', 'enriched with …' and 'proteins and nutrients'?

5 What effect is created by the use of 'It's your world – live it!' and 'be free'?

6 What is the effect of printing some words and phrases in italics and some entirely in capitals? Why are parts of the text in different sizes and type faces?

7 Consider the way the whole advertisement is put together: pictures, colour, type faces, headings and words. What sort of impression of the Franki Toiletries Range are you being given?

8 What sort of teenager is 'Franki' attempting to appeal to? Does 'Franki' appeal to you? What could have been added to this advertisement to make Franki more attractive to young people?

Learning about language: *more about nouns*

In Unit 2 you learned that:

- **a noun is a naming word**

- **nouns may be the name of a person, a thing, a place or an idea.**

Nouns may be grouped in other ways:

- **common nouns – nouns that name something general.**
  For example: pupil; car; valley; friendship

- **proper nouns – nouns that name something particular.**
  For example: Alison; Nissan Micra; Manchester
  (*Note: proper nouns are always given a capital letter.*)

- **concrete nouns – nouns that name something tangible,**
  i.e. something you can touch, see, hear or smell.
  For example: girl; car; castle; trumpet

- **abstract nouns – nouns that name things which are not tangible,** i.e. ideas, emotions.
  For example: greed; satisfaction; hatred; anger.

Skills practice: *recognising common and proper nouns*

Exercise A

Copy out these sentences. In each one, underline or highlight the common nouns. Give the proper nouns capital letters.

1 The mouse ran behind the chair.

2 Why do sarah and alison always argue?

3 We are spending our holiday in spain.

4 Other children like oranges and bananas.

5 The train from york arrived at king's cross dead on time.

6 Our class saw elephants, bears, snakes and many other animals during the visit to london zoo.

7 My favourite author is terry pratchett.

8 Where are the pictures of our weekend in edinburgh?

9 I've always been an arsenal supporter.

10 My friend shafiq is visiting his grandparents in pakistan.

Exercise B

Copy out these sentences. In each one, highlight or underline the concrete nouns in one colour and the abstract nouns in another.

1 My appointment with the dentist filled me with fear.

2 The sight of the daffodils gently swaying in the breeze filled me with happiness.

3 Tourism brings a lot of visitors to our town to see the ruined castle.

4 Who said, 'Peace with honour'?

5 Elephants may have a thick skin, but they are also known for their intelligence.

6 The arrival of the train from Birmingham has been delayed.

7 Success is its own reward.

8 We stayed in a little hotel overlooking the river.

9 Our friendship will last longer than just the next term.

10 The disturbance in the classroom stopped immediately as the headteacher appeared in the doorway.

Word building: *more noun suffixes*

In Unit 2, suffixes were used to make names for people who 'do things'. There are two more suffixes that can be used in the same way: **-eer** and **-ee**.

For example: someone who climbs mountains
is a 'mountain-eer' someone
who is absent is an 'absent-ee'

When the person who 'does things' is female, the ending **-ess** can be used.

For example: someone who acts may be an 'act-or' or an 'actr-ess'

There are many occasions, however, when this ending does not work. If it is necessary to emphasise that a doctor is female, the word **woman-** has to be added – woman-doctor.

However, it is now quite common for people to use the male form of the word to include both sexes.

For example: a female doctor would remain 'doctor', and
a female actress would remain 'actor'.

Skills practice: *creating nouns*

Exercise A

Add the suffixes –eer or –ee where appropriate to the following word stems to make nouns. The first one has been done for you as an example.

Stem	Noun formed with –eer/–ee
auction	*auctioneer*
chariot	
refer	
engine*	
refuge*	
employ	
election	
racket	
nominate*	
evacuate*	

(* Note spellings of the nouns you make!)

Exercise B

Add the suffix –ess to the following word stems to make feminine nouns. The first one has been done for you.

Stem	Noun formed with –ess
heir	heiress
lion	
priest	
god*	
host	
manager	
prince*	
tiger*	
duke*	
waiter*	

(* Note spellings of the nouns you make!)

Text building: *apostrophes*

Nouns are often linked together when someone or something belongs to another person or thing. **This link or idea of 'belonging to' is shown by the use of an apostrophe followed by the letter 's'.**

For example: Diane owns a car. It is **Diane's car**.
Our cat has long whiskers. They are the **cat's whiskers**.

Remember, 'the owner' gets the apostrophe plus 's' after its name. This is still true even if the 'owner' is more than one person, but in such cases, the 's' is dropped.

For example: If all the girls in the class were laughing, it would be described as 'the girls' laughter', i.e. the laughter is coming from the girls so the apostrophe is placed immediately after girls, but the 's' is not added.

The apostrophe is also used to indicate that a letter has been left out. For example, 'I am going on holiday' becomes

'I'm going on holiday' if 'am' is used in the shortened form. This omission of letters which are replaced by an apostrophe often occurs in writing down spoken language (see Unit 7).

Skills practice: *using apostrophes*

Exercise A
Make the following phrases shorter by using an apostrophe plus 's' to show possession.

For example: The dog which belongs to Nasim = Nasim's dog

1 the trunk of the elephant
2 the book belonging to Shabir
3 the homework done by Graham
4 the house where the twins live
5 the claws of the cat
6 the results gained by the pupils
7 the success of the children
8 the surprise for Mum
9 the question asked by Gary
10 the photograph of Bianca

Exercise B
Insert apostrophes, where necessary, to show letters omitted in words in the following sentences.

For example: Where's my pen?

1 He didnt want to play that game.
2 They cant do it in time.
3 Havent you finished yet?
4 Whats for tea?
5 I dont know the answer.
6 Whens the end of term party?
7 She wouldnt do as she was told.
8 Thats a silly idea!
9 You couldnt punch a hole in a paper bag!
10 Id like to see that film.

Writing

- Return to the beginning of this unit and look at the notes you made about revolting objects.

- Create a persuasive advertisement or information leaflet detailing the excellent and exclusive qualities of one or more of your chosen objects.

- What adjectives or nouns might be chosen to create a pleasant-sounding and/or exclusive image for your object? Perhaps it might help if you drew up a table with two columns, one headed 'actual words' and the other 'persuasive words', to focus your ideas.

- Think about how you might create a more attractive or positive image for whatever you have chosen. Look at the advertisement on page 41 and see if that suggests possible approaches. How could you use a combination of pictures, slogans and headings?

- Try to make an attractive visual impact so that people will want to read your detailed and delightful description of this remarkable object.

 ICT Extra!

Desktop publishing
Like the Business Studies group who produced the advertisement for 'Franki', explore your desktop publishing facilities to help produce a similar 'professional' looking advertisement.

Unit 6: Please note!

In this unit you will:

- read and make notes on a piece of writing;
- learn more about plural and collective nouns;
- learn more about using suffixes to form noun plurals;
- practise forming noun plurals;
- practise writing up notes.

Speaking and listening

- Working with a partner, each choose a well known person you admire (a rock star, a footballer or an actress, for example).

- Now write down ten facts you know about that person.

- Look at each list and discuss how you would turn this information into a short, informative article about your celebrity's life.

- Try to decide which of your short biographies might be the most interesting, and why.

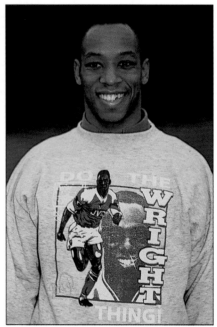

Understanding

You have just attempted to write up a set of notes about someone's life. Making notes can be difficult, but it is a valuable skill. When making notes you have to pick out the main facts or opinions that a writer or speaker is putting forward.

- Check back to Unit 2, where you practised picking out facts in an advertisement to answer questions.

- Now read this advertisement for a vacuum cleaner and write down ten things – in a list or note form – about it.

Make a clean sweep

If facing the cleaning makes you feel like a seven-stone weakling about to do battle with a boxing champ, it's time to get some power into your punch. For anyone can glide through housework like a gladiator with an Oreck XL lightweight vacuum with a Titan's strength.

Why wear yourself out in single combat against dust and grime when the Oreck workforce can be on your side?

Tough and reliable, the Oreck XL has the power to deliver a thoroughly professional clean. That's why more than 50,000 hotels, hospitals, airports, restaurants and offices worldwide won't use any other vacuum.

Yet the Oreck is still the lightest full-size vacuum cleaner available today. Weighing in at just eight-and-a-half pounds, it is light enough to be coaxed along by the palm of the hand. When you switch on the Oreck, it appears to weigh even less. The Oreck's superb  suction action creates a cushion between it and the floor surface, making it glide along, leaving only a freshly-cleaned pathway behind.

From the thickest pile carpets to bare boards, nothing beats the Oreck XL. Its specifically patented Microsweep action allows it to adjust automatically to all floor surfaces, where the machine's strong suction power continues to banish every trace of dust and dirt.

In fact, the dust-busting Oreck is so effective that it helps those who suffer from hay fever and other allergic reactions. As the Oreck greedily sucks in an amazing 275 cubic feet of air per minute, its special Celoc Hypo-Allergenic air filtration system ensures that irritating microscopic particles are not exhausted back into the room.

The Oreck XL has an ingenious top-fill design, so the filter bag holds much more than bottom-fill bags. And because the dirt is never disturbed in the bag when you turn it on, there's no filthy cloud of dust.

Once the dust is in the massive disposable eight-litre bag, it stays there. The bag's filtering material is specially treated to make sure germs and bacteria are destroyed.

Skills practice: *writing up notes*

■ On the left-hand side of the page are the notes used to produce the finished pieces of writing about environmental pollution shown on the right.

■ The final piece of writing should have three paragraphs; the first and third have been completed; you have to write the second.

■ Use the information in the notes; you need not add any other ideas of your own.

■ Concentrate on expressing the information clearly and logically, making sure you link your paragraph with the others.

Oil pollution

(Paragraph 1)
■ widely used in industry
■ 'natural' commodity
■ formed geologically, not man-made
■ extracted from the earth
■ results from build up and decomposition of tiny organisms
■ takes millions of years

(Paragraph 2)
■ hazardous when brought to surface
■ decays slowly when exposed to air
■ immediate effect is to contaminate land or water
■ possible distressing effect on birds' plumage
■ also on respiratory systems of fish
■ can damage coral reefs
■ dispersal often involves use of man-made, non-natural detergents
■ these may have severe long term environmental effects

(Paragraph 3)
■ detergents designed to reduce surface tension around oil droplets
■ makes it easier for oil and water to mix
■ disturbs chemistry of oxygen uptake by marine life
■ effect is to kill off water bodies very quickly

(Paragraph 1)

Oil is used widely in industry. It is a naturally occurring commodity, formed by geological processes without human intervention. It has to be extracted from the earth where it has formed as a result of the build up and partial decomposition of the bodies of microscopic organisms over a period of millions of years.

(Paragraph 2: to be written by you)

(Paragraph 3)

Detergents are designed to disperse oil slicks by reducing the surface tension around the oil droplets, thus allowing the oil and water to mix more easily. Unfortunately, this process disturbs the chemistry of the oxygen uptake by fish and other types of marine life. Consequently, water bodies may be killed off very rapidly.

Learning about language: *more about nouns*

In Unit 2 you learned that:

- **a noun is a naming word**
- **nouns may be the name of a person, a thing, a place or an idea.**

In Unit 5 you learned that nouns may be further subdivided into **common nouns** and **proper nouns**, **concrete nouns** and **abstract nouns**.

Nouns may also be subdivided into:

- **plural nouns – nouns that refer to more than one object, person, etc.**
  For example: dogs; sheep; children; women
- **collective nouns – nouns that are used as the name for a group.**
  For example: box (of nails); herd (of cattle); team (of players)

Skills practice: *recognising plural and collective nouns*

Copy out these sentences. In each one, underline or highlight the plural nouns in one colour and the collective nouns in another.

1 The crowd applauded wildly.
2 Thieves broke in while the owners were shopping.
3 When the shepherds entered the stable, they heard oxen lowing quietly outside.
4 Other children play happily together.
5 The committee finally rejected the proposal.
6 Our class saw elephants, bears, snakes and a pride of lions during our visit to the zoo.
7 Those sausages are burnt.
8 Where are the pictures of our first team?
9 Herds of bison used to roam the American plains.
10 If you want to join the choir, go to the music room.

Word building: *noun suffixes for making plural nouns*

The plural form of a noun is usually made by adding an 's' to the singular form.

For example: dog/dogs; house/houses; eye/eyes

However, there are a number of exceptions, many with their own rules.

■ **nouns ending with a 'y' following a vowel, form their plural in the usual way by adding an 's'.**
For example: donkey/donkeys; boy/boys; way/ways

■ **BUT nouns ending with a 'y' following a consonant, form their plural by dropping the 'y' and adding 'ies'.**
For example: baby/babies; lady/ladies; butterfly/butterflies

■ **Some nouns ending in 'f' or 'fe' form their plural in the usual way by adding an 's'.**
For example: cliff/cliffs; chief/chiefs; safe/safes

■ **BUT most nouns ending with an 'f' or 'fe' drop the 'f' or 'fe' and add 'ves'.**
For example: wolf/wolves; leaf/leaves; half/halves

(Other such words are: wife, life, knife, self, calf, shelf, loaf, thief, scarf, wharf, hoof and sheaf.)

■ **Nouns ending in 'o', 'ss', 'sh', 'ch' or 'x' usually form their plural by adding 'es'.**
For example: tomato/tomatoes; kiss/kisses; bush/bushes; pitch/pitches; suffix/suffixes

■ **A few nouns form their plural by a vowel change in the word stem.**
For example: man/men; woman/women; foot/feet; mouse/mice; louse/lice; goose/geese; tooth/teeth

■ **A few nouns which are names of animals do NOT change in the plural.**
For example: one sheep/two sheep; deer; grouse; trout; salmon

■ **Words which have Latin or Greek forms make their plurals according to Latin or Greek rules.**
For example: radius/radii; crisis/crises; memorandum/memoranda; index/indices

Skills practice: *creating plural nouns*

Exercise A
Give the plural form of the following singular nouns. The first one has been done for you as an example.

Singular	Plural
cousin	cousins
week	
teacher	
monkey	
chair	
day	
country	
sister	
fairy	
child*	

(* Watch out! This has a very irregular plural form!)

Exercise B
Give the plural form of the following nouns ending in –f and –fe. The first one has been done for you as an example.

Singular	Plural
knife	knives
wife	
loaf	
hoof	
shelf	
cliff	
life	
calf	
thief	
scarf	

Exercise C

Give the plural form of the following nouns ending in –o, –ss, –sh, –ch and –x. The first one has been done for you.

Singular	Plural
box	boxes
brush	
potato	
fox	
patch	
glass	
bench	
match	
bullrush	
ox*	

(* Watch out! This has a very irregular plural form!)

Exercise D

Give the plural form of the following nouns. The first one has been done for you.

Singular	Plural
man	men
mouse	
house	
grouse	
tooth	
oasis	
deer	
phenomenon	
goose	
axis	

Exercise E

Give the collective noun for each of the following. The first one has been done for you as an example. There is no simple rule about the nature of collective nouns. You will need to make use of dictionaries and/or encyclopedias to research the answers to this question.

Plural	Collective
lions	pride of lions
bees	
ships	
monkeys	
geese	
whales	
sheep	
hounds	
cows	
pups	

Text building: *writing up notes*

A pupil was given the following notes about Joanna Lumley, who plays the role of the chain-smoking, champagne-drinking Patsy in *Absolutely Fabulous.*

> *born India, 1946 – father an officer in Indian army – brought up in Far East – sent to boarding school in Sussex – did well at school – prefect's badge taken away for smoking*

These notes were written up as a short paragraph.

> Joanna Lumley was born in India in 1946. She was brought up in the Far East as her father was an officer in the Indian Army. As a girl, she was sent to a boarding school in Sussex where she did very well and became a prefect. However, she was caught smoking and her prefect's badge was taken away.

- Notice how the notes are turned into complete, grammatically correct sentences. Some of the ideas are linked to make the account more interesting.

- Compare this piece of writing with your own work at the start of this unit. Which is better?

 ICT Extra!

Finding information via the Internet
Use the Internet to find out more information about Joanna Lumley to add to your 'biography'. For example, use sites related to radio and television programmes, fan clubs and interviews.

Writing

- Here is some more information about Joanna Lumley.

- Use these notes as the basis for two more short paragraphs about her, one on her early career and one on more recent events in her life.

turned down by RADA — became a photographic model — worked for Jean Muir — appeared as a Bond girl in 'On Her Majesty's Secret Service' — was 'seventies action girl Purdey in 'The New Avengers' — appeared in 'Coronation Street' playing Ken Barlow's girlfriend — starred with David Callum in sci-fi series 'Sapphire and Steel'

1994 spent nine days alone on an uninhabited island for a BBC documentary — same year awarded honorary doctorate Kent University — 1996 Fellowship set up at Oxford in her name — keen environmentalist/animal rights campaigner — once marched on Downing Street with a piglet under her arm to complain about transportation of live animals — has written three books including autobiography 'Stare Back and Smile' — in 1997 retraced a journey across the Himalayas made by her grandparents in 1931

Unit 7: Spoken English

In this unit you will:

- think about the differences between spoken and written English;
- learn more about verbs and their tenses;
- practise forming different tenses;
- learn about and practise punctuating direct speech.

Speaking and listening

- Work in groups of three.
- Take turns to tape record a short piece of conversation between two of you, with the third operating the tape recorder. *(The operator should try to keep secret exactly which pieces of conversation are being recorded, because it is important for this exercise that the talk is 'natural' and not rehearsed.)*

- When each person has had a turn at recording, play back each of the short extracts and try to turn them into written dialogue or speech as if they were part of a story.
- List any problems you have writing things down.

Understanding

Writers use conversation to let the reader know what their characters think and to reveal aspects of their personalities. However, so much of what people say is communicated by tone of voice, looks and gestures – what is often called body language – and it is very difficult to write such things down. Also, in conversation, people often fail to complete sentences, or use words or phrases in isolation in a way that only makes sense in a face-to-face situation.

In your tape-recorded conversations, you have used 'spoken English', and in the extract that follows you will read 'written (or literary) spoken English'. It is important to understand the difference between these spoken forms of language and written English.

Now read this extract from the end of a short story called *The Lumber-Room* by Saki. Nicholas has contrived to get his cousins sent on an outing to Jagborough Cove so that, with the house to himself, he may explore the lumber-room. His aunt does not trust Nicholas and tries to keep an eye on him.

'Nicholas, Nicholas!' she screamed, 'you are to come out of this at once. It's no use trying to hide there; I can see you all the time.'

It was probably the first time for twenty years that anyone had smiled in that lumber-room.

5   Presently the angry repetitions of Nicholas' name gave way to a shriek, and a cry for somebody to come quickly. Nicholas shut the book, restored it carefully to its place in the corner, and shook some dust over it. Then he crept from the room, locked the door, and replaced the key exactly where he had found it. His aunt was

10 still calling his name when he sauntered into the front garden.

'Who's calling?' he asked.

'Me', came the answer from the other side of the wall; 'didn't you hear me? I've been looking for you in the gooseberry

15 garden, and I've slipped into the rain-water tank. Luckily there's no water in it, but the sides are slippery and I can't get out. Fetch the ladder from under the cherry tree …'

'I was told I wasn't to go into the

20 gooseberry garden,' said Nicholas promptly.

'I told you not to, and now I tell you that you may,' came the voice from the rain-water tank, rather impatiently.

'Your voice doesn't sound like aunt's,' objected Nicholas; 'you may be the Evil One tempting me to be disobedient. Aunt often

25 tells me that the Evil One tempts me and that I always yield.
This time I'm not going to yield.'

'Don't talk nonsense,' said the prisoner in the tank, 'go and
fetch the ladder.'

'Will there be strawberry jam for tea?' asked Nicholas innocently.

30   'Certainly there will be,' said the aunt, privately resolving
that Nicholas should have none of it.

'Now I know you are the Evil One and not aunt,' shouted
Nicholas gleefully. 'When we asked aunt for strawberry jam
yesterday she said there wasn't any. I know there are four jars of

35 it in the store cupboard, because I looked, and of course you
know it's there, but she doesn't, because *she* said there wasn't
any. Oh, Devil, you *have* sold yourself!'

There was an unusual sense of luxury in
being able to talk to an aunt as though one

40 was talking to the Evil One, but Nicholas
knew, with childish discernment, that such
luxuries were not to be over-indulged in.
He walked noisily away, and it was a
kitchen maid, in search of parsley, who

45 eventually rescued the aunt from the rain-
water tank.

Tea that evening was partaken of in a fearsome silence. The
tide had been at its highest when the children had arrived at
Jagborough Cove, so there had been no sands to play on – a

50 circumstance that the aunt had overlooked in the haste of
organising the punitive expedition. The tightness of Bobby's
boots had had disastrous effects on his temper the whole of the
afternoon, and altogether the children could not have been said
to have enjoyed themselves. The aunt maintained the frozen

55 muteness of one who has suffered undignified and unmerited
detention in a rain-water tank for thirty-five minutes.

1 What do we learn about Nicholas's aunt in this extract?

You should think about:

- what she says to Nicholas;
- the way she speaks to him;
- what she thinks privately.

2 What things have contributed to Nicholas's happiness at the end of this extract?

You should think about:

- the visit to the lumber-room;
- what happens to his aunt in the garden;
- the cousins' visit to Jagborough Cove;
- his overall view of things at the end of the day.

Look again at the transcripts and notes you made in the Speaking and listening activity and then answer this final question.

3 Compare the 'words spoken' by Nicholas in this extract with the transcript you have made of your tape-recorded talk. What differences do you notice between storybook dialogue and your own actual dialogue?

Many points might strike you, but you should think particularly about:

- sentence forms;
- interruptions/abbreviations/hesitations (e.g. 'Yeah'/'Me too'/ 'O.K.'/'Well, I ... er ... er');
- choice of words.

Learning about language: *more about verbs*

In Unit 3, you learned that:

- **A verb is a doing or action word.**

Verbs appear in many different forms, however, and it is important to distinguish between the different forms and the ways they are used.

For example, what is the difference between:

- I hear you.
- I heard you.
- I will hear you.

All three statements make it clear that the listener ('I') is able to hear the speaker ('you'). Yet the three forms of the verb 'hear' would occur in different situations.

Firstly, actions take place at different times: sometimes now, at this very moment; sometimes in the past and now finished; sometimes expected in the future.

The word 'tense' is used to describe the different forms verbs take to describe actions in the past, the present or the future:

- 'I hear you' describes what the listener ('I') is doing at the moment, (the present). The verb form 'hear' is in the **present tense**.

- 'I heard you' explains that the listener ('I') did hear whatever was said, but it happened some time ago in the past. The verb form 'heard' is in the **past tense**.

- 'I will hear you' is an indication that the listener ('I') will hear what the speaker has to say some time in the future. The verb form 'will hear' is in the **future tense**.

Skills practice: *recognising verb tenses*

Copy out these sentences. In each one underline or highlight the present, past and future tenses of the verbs in different colours.

1 I remembered my homework at the very last minute.
2 My mother will buy them for me tomorrow.
3 I made up my mind yesterday.
4 The other students are listening to me carefully.
5 I walked to school this morning, but tomorrow I will take the bus.
6 A flotilla of small ships accompanied the aircraft carrier into port.
7 The sausages are burning!
8 My class always sits quietly in assembly.
9 Please leave the room immediately.
10 I will attend to you later!

Word building: *verb suffixes for changing tenses*

- **The present tense of a verb usually consists of the verb stem, sometimes with an added '-s' or '-es' in the third person.**

  For example: I enjoy/you enjoy/she enjoys/we enjoy/they enjoy

- **In regular verbs, the simple past form is created by adding '-ed' to the verb stem (or '-d' when the verb ends in '-e') and is the same for first, second and third person forms.**

  For example: I enjoyed/you enjoyed/she enjoyed/we enjoyed/
  they enjoyed
  I asked/you asked/he asked/we asked/they asked

- **In all regular verbs, the simple future form is created by using an 'auxiliary verb' – 'shall' and 'will' – with the verb stem.**

  For example: I shall (will) enjoy/you will enjoy/she will enjoy/
  we shall (will) enjoy/they will enjoy
  I shall (will) ask/you will ask/he will ask/we shall
  (will) ask/they will ask

(Note: traditionally 'shall' was used in the 'I' and 'we' forms, but 'will' in all other cases. This is no longer the case.)

Skills practice: *using different tenses*

Exercise A
Complete these sentences with the correct version of the present tense of the verb. Look at the example.

> I (visit) my aunt every Tuesday.
> I visit my aunt every Tuesday.

1 I (believe) the children are still asleep.

2 Mum usually (drive) us home from school.

3 My father (bake) wonderful apple pies.

4 Grandma (hate) girls who wear too much make-up.

5 Rashid (play) cricket for the juniors.

6 Mum always (carry) an umbrella.*

7 I (love) chocolate cake.

   8 Rachel (study) history at university.*

   9 We always (wash) our hands before we eat.

10 Mr Green (teach) English.

   (* Take care over spelling with these words.)

Exercise B

Complete these sentences with the correct version of the past tense of the verb. Look at the example.

   I (visit) my aunt last Tuesday.
   I visited my aunt last Tuesday.

   1 I (believe) the children were still asleep.

   2 Mum (drive) us home from school yesterday.*

   3 My father (bake) a wonderful apple pie for supper last night.

   4 I (practise) all day for the last two days.

   5 Rashid (play) cricket for the juniors the other day.

   6 Mum always (carry) an umbrella.*

   7 I (love) that chocolate cake you brought into the office.

   8 Rachel (study) history at university until last summer.*

   9 We always (wash) our hands before eating if Mum was watching.

10 Mr Green (walk) home after his car broke down.

   (* Take care over spelling with these words.)

Exercise C

Complete these sentences with the correct version of the future tense of the verb. Look at the example.

   I (visit) my aunt next Tuesday.
   I shall visit my aunt next Tuesday.

   1 I (believe) the children are asleep when they are quiet.

   2 Mum (drive) us home from school tomorrow.

   3 My father (bake) a wonderful apple pie for supper tonight.

   4 I (practise) all day for the next two days.

   5 Rashid (play) cricket for the juniors the day after tomorrow.

   6 You (carry) an umbrella after that forecast if you have any sense.

   7 I (enjoy) that chocolate cake if you leave it in the office.

   8 Rachel (study) history at university for the next three years.

   9 We (wash) our hands before eating because Mum always checks up on us.

10 Mr Green (walk) home if his car breaks down.

Text building: *direct speech*

At the beginning of this unit you tried to turn a conversation into written language. Did you have any problems doing this? For example, in showing in written form what people might indicate by tone of voice or gestures when they are talking?

A lot of the extract from *The Lumber-Room* at the beginning of this unit consists of conversation between Nicholas and his aunt. This is set out using various punctuation devices, so the reader can 'hear' what the two characters are saying to each other.

'Direct speech' describes words that are actually spoken.

Look at the rules that are used:

1 **Words actually spoken are enclosed within speech/ quotation marks '……'.**

For example: **'Nicholas, Nicholas!'** she screamed …
'Who's calling?' he asked …

2 **The first spoken word has a capital letter** (even if it's not at the beginning of a sentence).

For example: '**Y**our voice doesn't sound like aunt's,' objected Nicholas.
She replied, '**D**on't talk nonsense …'

3 **The words spoken are separated from the rest of the sentence by a comma**; before (if the words spoken are not the beginning of the sentence), or after (if the words spoken do not end with a full stop, question mark or exclamation mark).

For example: … said the prisoner in the tank**,** 'go and fetch the ladder'.
'Me**,**' came the answer …
'Certainly there will be**,**' said the aunt …

but: 'Who's calling**?**' he asked …

4 **Begin a new paragraph every time there is a new speaker.**

For example: … aunt was still calling his name when he sauntered into the front garden.

'Who's calling?' he asked.

'Me,' came the answer from the other side of the wall …

Skills practice: *punctuating direct speech*

Set out this extract from *The Lumber-Room* correctly, adding the punctuation needed (including sentence markers).

> All the crying was done by his girl-cousin who scraped her knee rather painfully against the step of the carriage as she was scrambling in how she did howl said Nicholas cheerfully as the party drove off without any elation of high spirits that should have characterised it she'll soon get over that said the aunt it will be a glorious afternoon for racing about over those beautiful sands how they will enjoy themselves bobby won't enjoy himself much and he won't race either said Nicholas with a grim chuckle his boots are hurting him they're too tight why didn't he tell me they were hurting asked the aunt with some asperity he told you twice but you weren't listening you often don't listen when we tell you important things.

Writing

- Take one of the pieces of conversation you wrote down in the Speaking and listening task at the beginning of this unit.
- Build up the conversation into a full argument or discussion between the two people, making sure you follow the rules for setting out direct speech.
  (*Hint: first cut out anything that seems irrelevant and boring.*)

Unit 8: Sentence building

In this unit you will:

- read a short story about two girls shoplifting;
- learn more about verbs;
- learn more about creating different verb forms;
- learn about spelling rules and phrases.

Speaking and listening

This task is a group exercise, based on a very old children's game.

- Sit in a circle in groups of four or five and choose a leader.
- His/her job is to start a very simple story line (★ see below) which is passed on to the person to his/her left and so on round the circle.
- Each person has to add one more brief piece of information – a word, or a group of words – to the original sentence without making it too complicated.
- When the leader thinks the sentence has reached 'breaking point', stop the game and write out your group sentence.
- Your teacher can decide which group has produced the most interesting sentence.

★ For example:

Group leader: The girls sat in the café.

Second speaker: The two teenage girls sat in the café.

Third speaker: The two teenage girls sat drinking coffee in the café.

Fourth speaker: The two teenage girls sat drinking coffee in the busy city café.

Fifth speaker: The two teenage girls sat drinking coffee and talking about fashion in the busy city café.

Understanding

Read the following story and then answer the questions that follow. This is a second story about shoplifting (see Unit 3). Often similar subjects will be treated in very different ways by different writers.

The Bracelet

During the winter months, guided by the elder girl, the child began a deception that bothered her simply because she did not want to add further wrong-doing to her record. Sometimes on the occasional Saturday afternoon when Emily Baxter took her
5   to a movie, they did not return directly to Bluff Street afterwards but would loiter at the counters of Woolworths or Boots, lovingly fondling cosmetics, smelling samples of perfumes and unscrewing jar tops to stick their noses close to the cold cream inside. And they almost always ended up at the jewellery
10 counter! Urged on by her companion, the child became inordinately fond of a fine imitation gold bangle on which hung three small, delicate hearts of the same metal, and she dreamed of being given it on her birthday or at Christmas or hoped some unexpected windfall would enable her to buy it.
15   Emily Baxter liked a similar bracelet, and the child was surprised to see her wearing it one evening at Annette Durham's club meeting. Some precautionary flicker in the older girl's eyes kept her from exclaiming about it; but she was envious and felt cross that she could not be wearing the bracelet with the hearts,
20 which she already looked upon as her own and which she found much prettier.
        That Saturday as the two girls left the Princess Theatre, Emily Baxter seemed unusually eager to go 'shopping'. They passed through the store, smelling perfumes and opening jars and
25 saying, 'We're just looking,' when sales girls turned towards them expectantly. At the jewellery counter they lingered longer

continued …

than usual, and the child began to feel fretful. She also felt conspicuous because a man
30 passed them several times, apparently interested in what they might buy. When they left the store, it was cold and snowy and she was anxious to get
35 home. At the corner of Bluff Street and Western Avenue the older girl decided to separate from her charge.

'I'm late,' she said. 'Don't forget to tell your mother that we
40 saw the beginning again.'

'I won't,' the child said spitefully. 'I'll tell her that you wouldn't leave the store and that you take me there all the time. And I'll tell her that you left me here at the corner, and she won't like it a bit. She'll tell your mother.'

45 To her surprise the older girl was not angry or upset or argumentative, as she had expected.

'It's not really telling a lie,' she said. 'Besides, here is the bracelet you wanted. You can have it if you don't say what you said you would. Why do you want to spoil everything, anyway?'
50 But even though she chided, she smiled, and the child, overcome with gratitude, saw it as a friendly smile and trudged the short block through the snow, happily shaking the bracelet on her arm and listening to the fairy jingle of the tiny hearts.

Her mother was busy and paid little attention to her lateness,
55 nor did she notice the bracelet. On this night the West Side Cleaners was open late, besieged by telephone calls and annoyed customers waiting impatiently for garments, the delivery of which fell entirely to the boy so that his father could

60 stand the full evening at the hand iron. The doors were closed because of the cold, and the air in the shop was heavy with the smell of acetic acid and scorched canvas pressing cloths.

As much as the child disliked these odours, she preferred being here to being alone in the upstairs flat, from which she fled as rapidly as she could after she had washed the supper
65 dishes. When she re-entered the shop, she noticed a man talking with her mother, who sat with a suit jacket across her knees and several buttons lined up in the sewing machine. Her mother looked at her, but right through her, and her hands were trembling as she kept trying to thread a fine needle. The man
70 looked at the child, too, and nodded his head as she walked past. She didn't think that she knew him, but he seemed to know her, and as she leaned against the warm pad of the pressing machine, she wondered if it was the new insurance man, or the man to talk about installing electric lights upstairs,
75 as her father was always promising to do.

She heard the man say,

'I'm very sorry, Mrs Dunham, but that's the way it is. It happens all the time. In your case, because it's the first time, we won't do anything about it. Just thought you'd better know.
80 Could turn out to be pretty serious the next time …'

'I don't believe it,' her mother was saying over and over, and her voice trembled, and she talked some more of the time while the thread was in her mouth and she was trying to bite it off. 'A child who has everything that her father and I can give her. There
85 must be some mistake. It just couldn't have been Katherine!'

The man rose with a sigh. The girl eased her way to where she could see him as he said goodbye to her mother, who still sat fingering the thread and shaking her head, trying to make what he said not true. The man's hair was dark on the edge and
90 white where it was parted, and his dark blue suit was pressed

continued …

but very shiny. The cuffs of his overcoat sleeves were a little
frayed, and he looked tired, as though he had been on his feet
all day, and pale, as though he seldom went outside, and
unhappy, as though he had lived and relived the same scene
95 until he wanted no more of it.

'I've been to see the Baxter girl,' he said. 'I went there first
because, frankly, I hold her to blame. But – well, there you are.
Goodnight, Mrs Dunham,' and he opened the door of the shop
and went out, shoulders drooping, head lowered against the
100 cold wind.

Her mother sat for a long time after he had gone with her
hands in her lap. Then she threaded the needle with no trouble
and started sewing on a button. By now the child was
genuinely concerned. Whatever it was, she wanted it to be over
105 and finished before her father returned, because while
punishment from her mother was often quick and stinging, it
was never prolonged or cruel like the strap lashes of her father
in one of his worst moods. She moved to lean in the doorway
between the two rooms and cleared her throat.

110 Finally her mother said,

'Katherine, let me see the bracelet that you are wearing.' She
moved to her mother and extended her arm, glad for the respite.

'Emily gave it to me,' she said. 'We stopped after the
pictures today, and she bought it for me.'

115 Her mother looked at her pityingly.

'Don't lie, Katherine,' she said. 'Don't make it worse by lying!'
Her voice broke and tears spilled on to the jacket. She brushed
them away angrily, dropped the needle, took the child by the
shoulder, and shook her until both ribbons fell to the floor.

120 'Why did you do it?' she said. 'Why did you have to go and
disgrace your father and me by stealing? Why? Why?'

(from *A Touch of Innocence* by Katherine Dunham)

Now answer these questions:

1 Why did the two girls not go straight home from the movie?

2 What cover-up story did they use to explain their lateness?

3 Why was the younger girl worried by the deception?

4 How did the girl dream of getting the bracelet?

5 Why did the younger girl say she would 'tell' on Emily?

6 Why did Emily give her the bracelet?

7 Emily says, 'It's not really telling a lie.' What does this tell us about Emily?

8 Why isn't the girl worried when she enters the shop and finds the man there?

9 When does the girl begin to realise she is in trouble?

10 The writer gives various details about the man's appearance. What do these tell us about him and his job?

11 How does Katherine's mother react to what the man tells her?

12 How does she react to what Katherine says?

13 What is your opinion about the way Katherine's mother treats her?

14 What do you think Katherine's feelings are towards her mother at the end of the extract?

15 What answer do you think could be given to Katherine's mother's question, 'Why did you do it?'

Now re-read the extract about Joby and Gus in Unit 3 (pages 25–26) and write an account of the different ways in which a shoplifting incident is handled by the two writers.

You should think about all aspects of the two texts, but you might particularly comment on:

- characters;
- how the situation (time and place) is introduced;
- the pace of development of what happens;
- sentence structures and use of dialogue;
- how the stories end (although the *Joby* episode is an extract).

Learning about language: *more about verb forms*

In Unit 7, which looked at verb tenses, you saw that regular verbs form their past tense by adding the suffix '-ed' to the word stem. You also saw that **some verbs are irregular** and form the past tense in other ways.

For example: She shut the door.
           not   She shutted the door.

           He caught the ball.
           not   He catched the ball.

           I felt happy.
           not   I feeled happy.

Irregular verbs do not follow the rules. You just have to learn all their irregular forms as you come across them!

The exercises in the Skills practice section divide some of the commoner ones into different groups to help you.

Skills practice: *forming the past tense of irregular verbs*

Exercise A
This concentrates on irregular verbs like 'shut', which use the same form for the present and the past tense.

Copy out and complete these sentences, choosing from this list:
  read   shut   burst   put   cut   let   hurt   bet   set   split

1 Asifa _____ her hand and so I took her to the hospital.

2 I _____ David ten pence that Ian would be late for school yesterday.

3 I _____ a super book last week.

4 The other children _____ out laughing when I said that to the teacher.

5 At the end of the lesson, we walked out in silence and Miss Edwards _____ the door very quietly.

6 'Have you _____ my things away?'

7 When he threatened me, I _____ him have it.

8 Mr Green _____ double homework yesterday.

9 After the burglary, the criminals _____ their haul three ways.

10 What Wesley said really _____ my feelings.

Exercise B

This focuses on irregular verbs like 'catch', which form the past tense by changing the vowel (and sometimes the final consonants) in the stem.

Copy out and complete these sentences, using the past tense of the verb stem given.

1 Jenny (ride) her horse across the field.

2 We (run) home as fast as we could when it started to rain.

3 I (write) 'thank you' letters to both my aunts after my birthday.

4 None of the children (speak), they were so frightened.

5 At the end of assembly, we (sing) a carol and then (break) up for Christmas.

6 Who (take) my things out of this bag?

7 Michael (fly) home from his holiday in Spain.

8 Laura (tell) her father she had been selected for the first team.

9 I (see) Halley's Comet the other night.

10 He (swim) right across the lake.

Exercise C

This focuses on irregular verbs like 'feel', which form the past tense by changing the vowel(s) in the stem and adding a final –t.

Copy out and complete these sentences, using the past tense of the verb stem given.

1 'Look! I (mean) what I said!'

2 Owen (leave) immediately the concert was over.

3 I (sweep) up the leaves and put them on the bonfire.

4 The other children held a collection and (buy) Darren a present.

5 Emma thinks she (lose) her necklace in the garden.

6 'Have you (think) of anything yet?'

7 The cat (creep) silently along the wall, stalking the mouse.

8 'Has anyone (bring) an apple for lunch?'

9 Lee (deal) the cards and the game started.

10 Rhani (leap) out of the chair in amazement.

(Note: the truth is that there are so many exceptions to the rule with irregular verbs, you just have to be careful with each one and learn the forms you don't already know.)

Word building: *spelling rules: 'i' before 'e'*

In previous units you learned how to make different word forms by adding various suffixes to the word stem.

These changes often affect the spelling of the stem and sometimes mean that adding the suffix is not always straightforward.

These spelling rules will help your word building.

Rule 1: The rule: 'i' before 'e' except after 'c' (but only in those words where the 'i' and 'e' together make a long 'e' sound, as in 'keen')

For example: bel**ie**f; th**ie**f　　(long 'e' sound, so 'i' before 'e')

rec**ei**ve; c**ei**ling　(long 'e' sound after 'c', so 'e' before 'i')

l**ei**sure; **ei**ght　　(no long 'e' sound, so 'e' before 'i')

Rule 2: Some words do not obey the rule.

For example: s**ei**ze; counterf**ei**t; caff**ei**ne; prot**ei**n; plus (depending on how you pronounce them) **ei**ther and n**ei**ther

Rule 3: In words with 'cie' (e.g. efficient) **where the 'ci' makes a 'sh' sound, 'i' comes before 'e'.**

For example: suffi**cie**nt; an**cie**nt

Rule 4: Where the 'i' and the 'e' make separate sounds (e.g. aud**ie**nce) **the spelling follows the pronunciation – 'i' before 'e'.**

For example: soc**ie**ty; sc**ie**ntific

Skills practice: *words with 'i' and 'e' together*

Exercise A
Complete these words with the correct spelling, using Rule 1.
The first has been done for you as an example.

rel _ _ f	*relief*
th _ _ r	
f _ _ ld	
br _ _ f	
n _ _ ghbour	
for _ _ gn	
p _ _ ce	
h _ _ ght	
d _ _ sel	
v _ _ n	

Exercise B
Complete these words with the correct –ie– or –ei– spelling.
The first has been done for you.

ach _ _ ve	*achieve*
s _ _ ze	
w _ _ ght	
n _ _ ce	
prot _ _ n	
conven _ _ nt	
conc _ _ ve	
n _ _ ther	
gr _ _ f	

Text building: *phrases*

Look at the sentences you wrote in the sentence building game at the start of this unit. Each person in your group is likely to have added a word or **phrase** to the original simple sentence.

■ **A phrase is a small group of words which make sense as a unit, but are not a sentence** (see Unit 1) **or a clause** (see Unit 9). Phrases do not usually include a verb, unless they are verb phrases (explained in Unit 9).

This section will consider noun and adjective phrases; you have already learned about nouns and adjectives in previous units. In later units you will also learn about verb, adverbial and prepositional phrases.

- **A noun phrase is a group of words linked together to act as a noun.**

For example: **The Head of Lower School** conducted assembly this morning.

The lads were hanging about at **the corner of the street**.

- **An adjective phrase is a group of words, beginning with or containing an adjective, linked together to act as an adjective. It is a more complicated way of describing something.**

For example: Nicky was as **miserable as sin** that morning.

If you believe you can get away with that, you're **amazingly stupid**.

Skills practice: *identifying noun and adjective phrases*

Exercise A
Copy out these sentences, highlighting or underlining the noun phrases.

1 Mrs Wright's class was really enjoying history for once.
2 The rush hour traffic delayed me by nearly an hour.
3 The garden gate was swinging on its hinges.
4 Fiona had a blob of cream on the end of her nose.
5 The children from next door are always climbing into our garden.
6 Holidaymakers from France were crowding onto the ferry.
7 Forgetting your games kit means detention at lunch time.
8 A gang of men started digging up the road.
9 I looked up and saw a flock of birds flying overhead.
10 A brand new car had crashed into the lamp-post at the end of the road.

Exercise B
Copy out these sentences, highlighting or underlining the adjective phrases.

1 The class all thought the work was tiring and tedious.

2 Cold and frightened, I hid behind the shed.

3 By the time we stopped walking, we were all really thirsty.

4 Her voice was almost inaudible because of the racket from outside.

5 The houses, dim, dingy and crowded together, had all their windows broken.

6 Warm and welcoming, the light pierced through the surrounding shadows.

7 Martin was as good as gold when he was with his grandmother.

8 The bird, ready for flight at any moment, watched the cat cross the lawn.

9 Worn out and drained of anger, I picked myself up and slunk away.

10 Your present looks bigger than mine.

Writing

Think back to the sentences your group created at the beginning of this unit. It's quite likely that many of you extended the original sentence by adding on noun or adjective phrases.

■ Below are six simple sentences. Try to develop them into more complex and interesting statements by adding extra words and phrases.

■ Then build a story around them so that each sentence becomes part of your story.

■ You may use the sentences in any order.

● **The lighthouse stood at the edge of the cliff.**
● **A boat was being thrown about by the waves.**
● **A steep path led down to the shore.**
● **There was only an old woman in sight.**
● **It started raining.**
● **A Land Rover drove up to the lighthouse.**

(Note: when you have completed a first draft of your story put it to one side, because in the next unit you will have a chance to develop it further.)

Unit 9: Inventing the future

In this unit you will:

- read an extract from a story about the future;
- learn more about verb tenses;
- learn and practise spelling patterns;
- learn about clauses.

Speaking and listening

- Working in groups of four or five, decide what would be the most helpful learning aids for pupils to have at school in 20 years' time.

- Choose the five best ideas and try to work out some design features.

- This unit is about the future, so let your imagination go and think of some really interesting inventions!

Understanding

Science fiction writers often choose words to create an impression of a world very different from the one we know today.

Read this passage, which imagines improvements to agricultural machinery in the future. Then answer the questions on page 84.

Men and Machines

This story is set in the far future, when all work is done by machines, which can think for themselves and function unattended, although they still rely on basic instructions from men. One day, however, the field-minder machine on an agricultural station finds the other machines completely disorganised.

> Steering carefully past them, the field-minder moved over to
> Warehouse Three and spoke to the seed distributor, which stood
> idly outside.
>   'I have a requirement for seed potatoes,' it said to the
> 5 distributor, and with a quick internal motion punched out an

order card specifying quantity, field number and several other
details. It ejected the card and handed it to the distributor.

The distributor held the card close to its eye and then said,

'The requirement is in order; but the store is not yet unlocked.
10 The required seed potatoes are in the store. Therefore I cannot
produce the requirement.'

Increasingly of late there had been breakdowns in the
complex system of machine labour, but this particular hitch had
not occurred before. The field-minder thought, then it said,

15   'Why is the store not yet unlocked?'

'Because Supply Operative Type P has not come this morning.
Supply Operative Type P is the unlocker.'

The field-minder looked squarely at the seed distributor,
whose exterior chutes and scales and grabs were so vastly
20 different from field-minder's own limbs.

continued …

'What class brain do you have, seed distributor?' it asked.

'I have a Class Five brain.'

'I have a Class Three brain.'

Therefore I am superior to you. Therefore I will go and see why
25 the unlocker has not come this morning.'

The field-minder approached it.

'I can do no more work until Warehouse Three is unlocked,' it
told the unlocker. 'Your duty is to unlock the
warehouse every morning. Why have you not unlocked the
30 warehouse this morning?'

'I had no orders this morning,' replied the unlocker.
'I have to have orders every morning. When I have orders I
unlock the warehouse.'

'None of us has had any orders this morning,' a pen-propeller
35 said, sliding towards them.

'Why have you had no orders this
morning?' asked the field-minder.

'Because the radio issued none,'
said the unlocker, slowly rotating
40 a dozen of its arms.

'Because the radio station in the
city was issued with no
orders this morning,' said
the pen-propeller.

45   And there you had the
distinction between a Class
Six and a Class Three brain,
which was what the unlocker
and the pen-propeller possessed
50 respectively. All machine brains
worked with nothing but logic,
but the lower the class of
brain – Class
Ten being the lowest – the
55 more literal and less informative
answers to questions tended to be.

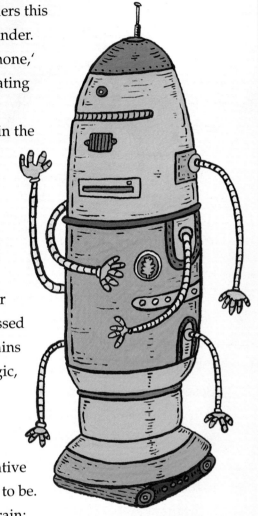

'You have a Class Three brain;
I have a Class Three brain,' the field-minder said to the pen-
propeller. 'We will speak to each other. This lack of orders is
60 unprecedented. Have you any
further information on it?'

'Yesterday orders came from the city. Today no orders have
come. Yet the radio has not broken down. Therefore they have
broken down ...' said the little pen-propeller.

65   'The men have broken down?'

'All the men have broken down.'

'That is a logical deduction,' said the field-minder.

continued ...

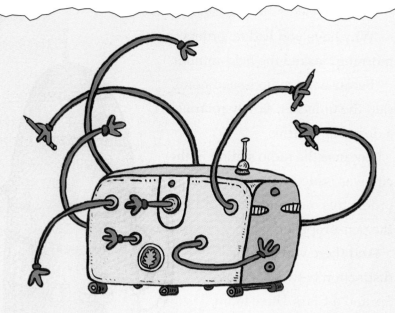

'That is the logical deduction,' said the pen-propeller. 'For if a machine had broken down it would have been quickly
70 replaced. But who can replace a man?'

While they talked, the unlocker, like a dull man at a bar, stood close to them and was ignored.

'If all the men have broken down, then we have replaced Man,' said the field-minder, and he and the pen-propeller eyed
75 one another speculatively. Finally the latter said, 'Let us ascend to the top floor to find if the radio operator has fresh news.'

'I cannot go because I am too large,' said the field-minder. 'Therefore you must go alone and return to me. You will tell me if the radio operator has fresh news.'

80 'You must stay here,' said the pen-propeller. 'I will return here.' It skittered across to the lift. Although no bigger than a toaster, its retractable arms numbered ten and it could read as quickly as any machine on the station.

The field-minder waited patiently, not speaking to the
85 unlocker, which still stood aimlessly by. Outside a rotovator hooted furiously. Twenty minutes elapsed before the pen-propeller came back, hustling out of the lift …

'What information did you receive from the radio operator?' asked the field-minder.

90 'The radio operator has been informed by the operator in the city that all men are dead.'

The field-minder was momentarily silent, digesting this.

'All men were alive yesterday!' it protested.

'Only some were alive yesterday. And that was fewer than the 95 day before yesterday. For hundreds of years there have only been a few men, growing fewer.'

'We have rarely seen a man in this sector.'

'The radio operator said a diet deficiency killed them,' said the pen-propeller. 'He says that the world was once over 100 populated, and then the soil was exhausted in raising adequate food. This has caused the diet deficiency.'

'What is a diet deficiency?' asked the field-minder.

'I do not know. But that is what the radio operator said, and he is a Class Two brain.'

105 They stood there silent in the weak sunshine. The unlocker appeared in the porch and was gazing at them yearningly, rotating its collection of keys.

'What is happening in the city now?' asked the field-minder at last.

110 'Machines are fighting in the city now,' said the pen-propeller.

'What will happen here now?' asked the field-minder.

'Machines may begin fighting here too. The radio operator wants us to get him out of his room. He has plans to communicate with us.'

115 'How can we get him out of his room? That is impossible.'

'To a Class Two brain, little is impossible,' said the pen-propeller. 'Here is what he tells us to do …'

(From *Who Can Replace a Man?*, a short story by Brian Aldiss)

Now answer the following questions:

1 How large a machine was the field-minder? What evidence is there about its size?

2 Describe briefly the appearance of (a) the seed distributor, (b) the unlocker and (c) the pen-propeller. Which words or phrases give essential clues to their appearance?

3 Describe the differences between the various classes of brain. What was the lowest class of brain? What class of brain did each of the following have: (a) the field-minder, (b) the seed distributor, (c) the unlocker, (d) the pen-propeller and (e) the radio operator?

4 Why did the different machines have different types of brain?

5 What is the greatest difference between man and machines, even advanced machines such as those portrayed in this story?

6 How far is it possible or useful for people to be put into categories according to their intelligence, in the way the machines were? Give reasons to support your view.

7 For which job, at present done by you, would you most like to invent a machine?

8 Throughout history, people have been anxious about being put out of work when new machines have taken over jobs previously performed by man. Is this an argument for not inventing more machines? Explain what you think about this.

9 How does the writer's choice of words and the way sentences are formed help to create an impression of a world dominated by machines?

Learning about language: *more about verb forms*

Unit 7, dealing with verb tenses, explained the difference between verbs that describe present, past or future events. In English, however, there are **three forms of the present tense, three of the past tense** and **two of the future tense**.

| **The simple present:** | I work hard. |
| **The continuous present:** | I am working hard. |

The emphatic present:	I do work hard.
The simple past:	I worked hard.
The continuous past:	I was working hard.
The emphatic past:	I did work hard.
The simple future:	I shall/will work hard.
The continuous future:	I shall/will be working hard, *or* I am going to work hard.

Present tense

■ The **simple present** tense is usually used to express actions that are habitual (i.e. happen all the time).

For example: She smokes.
Cats drink milk.

■ The **continuous present** is usually used to express actions happening now.

For example: It is raining.
He is wearing a coat.

■ The **emphatic present** is usually used to give emphasis to actions that are habitual (i.e. happen all the time).

For example: I do watch sport.
You do like sweets.

Past tense

■ The **simple past** tense is usually used to express actions that ended at a definite time in the past.

For example: I met him yesterday.
He stopped running.

■ The **continuous past** is usually used to express past actions which continued for some time.

For example: They were cooking.
It was raining last night.

■ The **emphatic past** is usually used to emphasise actions that ended at some point in the past.

For example: I did wash up.
You did take it.

Future tense

■ The **simple future** tense is usually used to talk about actions that will take place in the future.

For example: I shall/return tomorrow.
They will wait.

■ The **continuous future** is usually used in the same way as the simple future, to express actions which are expected to take place.

For example: We will be meeting him next week.
He will be sitting his exam at the end of term.

■ Sometimes, however, the tone of voice can suggest a more definite intention to make something happen, and so this form also serves the purpose of the **emphatic future**.

For example: We will (definitely) be meeting him next week.
He will (no choice!) be sitting his exam at the end of term.

■ Or you can express emphasis in another way:

For example: We certainly will be meeting him next week.

Skills practice: *using simple, continuous and emphatic verb forms*

Exercise A
Copy out and complete these sentences using, as indicated, the simple, continuous or emphatic present tense forms of the verb stem given.

1 I (read) a play by Shakespeare. *(continuous)*
2 She (teach) French and German at the Sixth Form College. *(simple)*
3 They (wear) their coats because it's so cold. *(continuous)*
4 Shane (prefer) writing stories to doing exercises. *(simple)*
5 You really (like) tennis and cricket. *(emphatic)*
6 Rahila always (speak) very quietly. *(simple)*
7 I (write) my diary in bed just before I put the light out. *(simple)*
8 We (wait) for the bus into town. *(continuous)*
9 Peter is not shy; he (ask) questions in class. *(emphatic)*
10 Talk quietly because the baby (sleep) peacefully at last. *(continuous)*

Exercise B

Copy out and complete these sentences using the simple, continuous or emphatic past tense forms of the verb stem given.

1 I (live) in London for over five years. *(simple)*
2 They (drive) through town when they heard the explosion. *(continuous)*
3 At nine o'clock, he (walk) to work. *(continuous)*
4 We (watch) the match on television. *(simple)*
5 Liz always (try) her hardest in maths. *(emphatic)*
6 The thieves (hide) as the police car went slowly down the street. *(simple)*
7 My father certainly (take) the tube yesterday morning. *(emphatic)*
8 You (tell) me about Steve's illness before the phone rang. *(continuous)*
9 We (rush) across the room and flung our arms round Grandma. *(simple)*
10 He (chase) me when he fell over and cut his knee. *(continuous)*

Exercise C

Copy out and complete these sentences using the simple, continuous or emphatic future tense forms of the verb stem given.

1 I (know) tomorrow. *(simple)*
2 Tom (chop) some wood for the fire later. *(simple)*
3 I (visit) Paris in the spring and can arrange a meeting then. *(continuous)*
4 The train at platform 7 (depart) in ten minutes. *(simple)*
5 Dean definitely (leave) school on his sixteenth birthday. *(emphatic)*
6 The Teletubbies (return) to television in a new series next year. *(simple)*
7 We (look) for someone with good qualifications and experience when we make the appointment. *(continuous)*
8 I (speak) to your parents about your behaviour at the meeting next Wednesday. *(emphatic)*
9 Scott (come) to your party on Saturday. *(continuous)*
10 You (work) in this office under Mrs Dawson's supervision. *(simple)*

Word building: *spelling rules: a final 'y'*

- **Rule 1: With verbs ending in 'y', preceded by a consonant, the final 'y' changes to 'i' before any suffix, except '–ing'.**

For example: cry   crying   cried
                marry   marrying   married

This rule of 'the preceding consonant' also applies to forming the third person singular of the simple present and simple past tenses of verbs, and in forming the plural of nouns. The final '–y' is changed to '–ies' or '–ied'.

For example: cry   cries
                study   studied
                lady   ladies
                baby   babies

- **Rule 2: With verbs ending in 'y', preceded by a vowel, the final 'y' remains unchanged before any suffix.**

For example: stay   staying   stayed
                play   playing   played

This rule of 'the preceding vowel' also applies to forming the third person singular of the simple present tense of verbs and in forming the plural of nouns. The final '–y' remains unchanged and '–s' is simply added.

For example: buy   buys
                enjoy   enjoys
                key   keys
                day   days

These two rules also apply in most instances when a suffix is added to a word stem ending in '–y', i.e. with a preceding consonant the final '–y' changes to '–i' before the suffix; with a preceding vowel, just add the suffix.

For example: merry   merriment
                joy   joyful
                glory   glorious
                betray   betrayal

Skills practice: *words ending in −y*

Exercise A
Complete these words with the correct spelling, using Rule 1.
The first one has been done for you as an example.

multiply (3rd person singular present)	*multiplies*
terrify (3rd person singular past)	
heavy (add −ness)	
busy (add −ly)	
qualify (3rd person singular past)	
bury (add −al)	
hurry (3rd person singular present)	
sixty (add −th)	
victory (plural)	
ally (add −ance)	
vary (add −able)	

Exercise B
Complete these words with the correct spelling, using Rule 2.
The first one has been done for you.

pray (3rd person singular present)	*prays*
spray (3rd person singular past)	
pay (add −ment)	
employ (add −able)	
stray (3rd person singular past)	
boy (add −ish)	
delay (3rd person singular present)	
grey (add −er)	
way (plural)	
annoy (add −ance)	
destroy (add −able)	

Text building: *verb phrases and clauses*

In Unit 8, you learned about groups of words that form noun
and adjective phrases. In this unit you have learned that there are
verb forms – 'will be going', 'was watching', 'did listen' etc. –
which are made up of more than one word.

■ **A sequence of words taken together to make up one verb 'unit' is called a verb phrase.**

For example: In the sentence, 'When I awoke, I realised I must have been dreaming', 'awoke' and 'realised' are both verbs, but 'must have been dreaming' is a whole 'verb unit'. This is a **verb phrase**.

■ **The word 'clause' describes a group of words which contain a verb or verb phrase.**

Clauses are usually longer than phrases, but not as long as sentences.

For example: '... although he is over 50 now ...'

Often sentences will include more than one clause.

For example: '... although she is extremely beautiful, and possibly because she is also very intelligent ...'

■ Sentences always have a **main clause**, but some more complicated sentences also include one or more **subordinate clauses**.

For example: He was extremely rude to his tutor, but despite the fact that he was sent to the Head of Year, he still wasn't put in detention, although he did have to take home a report to his parents about the incident.

■ **The main clause has one verb, is the main 'idea' of the sentence and usually makes sense by itself – like a simple sentence.**

For example: The sentence 'Her husband is a teacher' is a simple sentence. The main clause is the only clause.

The sentence 'Her husband, who is older than me, is a teacher' is a more complicated sentence. It consists of a main clause – 'Her husband is a teacher' – and a subordinate clause – 'who is older than me'.

The sentence 'Her husband, who is older than me, is a teacher at the school that was built three years ago' is even more complex. However, it still contains the same main clause, but has a second subordinate clause – 'at the school that was built three years ago' – as well as the previous subordinate clause – 'who is older than me'.

■ **Subordinate clauses add to information in the main clause. They do not make sense on their own, even though they contain a verb.**

Skills practice: *identifying main and subordinate clauses*

Exercise A
Copy out these sentences and highlight or underline the main clause.

1 They stared at the pictures which reminded them so much of home.

2 The great sailing ships rushed up the Channel, driven on by the prevailing winds.

3 The flowers, that bloomed so well in the spring, were fading fast.

4 Sam, who was always the brave one, knocked on the door.

5 The monkeys screamed excitedly when they saw the keepers bringing their food.

6 We found ourselves in a weird cave, piled high with wooden crates.

7 When I had finally finished telling the headteacher what had happened, I returned to my classroom.

8 As I carried the plate into the dining room, I tripped over the carpet.

9 Before opening the letter, I studied the envelope carefully.

10 Just as I looked up, there was a loud explosion.

Exercise B

Copy out these sentences and highlight or underline the subordinate clauses.

1 It was nearly evening before I had climbed to the top of that hill.
2 My talk, which lasted ten minutes, was well received.
3 The room was filled by a strange noise that echoed through my head.
4 The old woman sat in her chair, while the children played on the floor.
5 I lay on my bed as the sound of music crashed through the open window.
6 The new pupil smiled as he was introduced to the rest of the gang.
7 The sun, which was now directly overhead, was scorching hot.
8 The present, which was wrapped in attractive silvery paper, was lying under the tree.
9 We looked up in surprise when we heard Robbie's shout.
10 I knew I was in the south of the country because the land was flat and unattractive.

Writing

- Return to the first draft of the piece of writing you did at the end of Unit 8.

- Think back to the sentences you started with and now try to make them more complex and interesting by turning some phrases into clauses and adding extra words.

- When you have finished, draft a final version.

- Finally, proof-read it for 'slips of the pen' and write it up.

Unit 10: Put a comma in it!

In this unit you will:

- read about Bologna in Italy;
- learn more terms for describing verb forms;
- learn about and practise more spelling patterns;
- learn about and practise the use of commas.

Speaking and listening

- A party of pupils of your age from your twin/exchange school in France will be spending a week in your area. They need a planned programme for five days during their stay.

- In groups of four or five, plan how you would entertain them for a day. Don't suggest anything too expensive, but make sure they get some flavour of what life is like in your part of the country. They won't want to spend all their time sightseeing or visiting museums!

- Keep notes of your ideas for the writing task at the end of this unit.

Understanding

Sometimes you will need to demonstrate your understanding of material by using it or interpreting it to create a plan of action. Read these two articles about the attractions of Bologna in Italy.

BREAKAWAY

BOLOGNA ON A PLATE

Jacky Smith tastes the delights of an Italian city that's far from the tourists' beaten track

As Italian cook Marcella Hazan points out, Bologna is "probably the only city in Italy that is instantly associated in the Italian mind not with monuments, nor with a heroic past, but with food".

A clear promise of some serious self-indulgence.

But what dazzles is the rosy beauty of the place. Bologna, after all, is not a "tourist" city. It's never mentioned in the same breath as Florence or Venice on the Grand Cultural Circuit. However, it does have its fair share of history ... they had a little difficulty back in the Middle Ages when a tide of students flooded the housing market. They came to study at the oldest university in Italy, which pre-dates such upstarts as Oxford and Cambridge. The locals solved the housing problem with mile upon mile of colonnades, snaking through the town centre, curve upon elegant curve. The students, from the 12th century on, lived above them and now the Bolognese carry out their daily round under these lovely arcades, which make Bologna one of the great cities to explore on foot.

Today's tourists don't seem to know about it – there's not a backpack in sight. This is due, I suspect, to a blessed lack of "must see this, don't miss that" highlights. The art of this city *is* the city. Sightseeing involves

The city of Bologna offers many varied and beautiful sights.

nothing more than wandering the streets. Begin with the colours. The Bolognese palette ranges from terracotta to ochre and saffron with a dash of paprika. It is obvious that it has always been a prosperous place, one that has been restored sympathetically from the Renaissance onwards. Bologna is an easy city for the casual visitor. There's no need to make timetable expeditions to see the best because every curve reveals a gem. Almost by accident, we walked down the Via Dell' Indipendenza towards the Piazza Maggiore, the theatre of the city. We became familiar with the tipsy medieval towers of Asinelli and

Garisenda, all that's left of the 180 or so that once ruled the skies. The easiest sightseeing of all, of course, is done from a café. But we did abandon the Camparis for the lovely Basilica of San Petronio and the churches of Santo Stefano. In the mood for intimations of mortality? Ask the porter for admission to the old anatomy theatre at the Palazzo dell' Archiginnasio, then come back to life in the sumptuous, extravagant markets off the Via Clavature and the Via Ugo Bassi. They inspire greed and reverence in equal proportions. The most inspirational food shops are in and around the Via Caprarie and provide a powerful cultural experience.

The same could and should be said for eating in Bologna. Without breaking the bank, we didn't have one dud meal. Indeed, the simplest place proved the best value. It was Fantoni (Via Del Pratello). We arrived, appetites sharpened by the market, and had a marvellous lunch, followed by a gentle walk home through the arched arcades.

On an escapist weekend when time is short, you want everything to work. The Baglioni is possibly the most elegant hotel in Bologna but we liked the Star Hotel Milano Excelsior and its smaller cousin, Alexander, next door. They are business hotels, directly opposite the railway station. That might not sound an advantage, but consider this – the airport bus collects and delivers from across the road. And, by train, Florence and Parma are a mere hour away; Venice two hours. Our day trip to Florence cost about £6 each and it was worth every lira. The journey was a joy, the day an aesthetic treat. But best of all was the return to tourist-free Bologna. It felt very much like paradise regained. ∎

TRAVEL FACTS

Italian Escapades, 227 Shepherd's Bush Road, London W6 7AS, 0181–748–2661, offer weekend packages to both the Star Hotel Milano Excelsior (£40 per person per night, bed and breakfast) and the Star Hotel Alexander (£30). From 1 March the prices rise to £46 and £38 respectively. Scheduled return flights cost £159. General information is available from the Italian State Tourist Office, 1 Princes Street, London W1R 8AY, 0171–408–1254. Sightseeing: don't miss the view from Asinelli tower. Art lovers should head for the Pinacoteca Nazionale (Via delle Belle Arti) and the Tapestry Museum (Via Barberia). Don't forget that most churches are closed from 12 noon until 3–3.30 pm; many museums open only in the morning and are closed on Mondays. Have a supply of 100 lire coins handy for lighting church frescos. The Tourist Office is in Pizza Maggiore, (010 39) 51 23 96 60.

Markets: Mercato Ugo Bassi (Via Ugo Bassi) is a vast indoor market. An outdoor market takes place on Via Pescherie, off Piazza Maggiore. Both open Mon–Wed 7.15 am–1 pm and 5–7 pm; Fri 7 am–1 pm and 4.30–7.30 pm; Thurs and Sat 7.15 am–1 pm.

Books: Blue Guide to Northern Italy (A & C Black, £19.99). Let's Go 98: Italy (Macmillan, £12.99).

(Article by Jacky Smith, from *Homes and Gardens*, February 1994)

Bologna

Emilias's capital, Bologna, is a boomtown of the eighties whose computer-associated industries have brought conspicuous wealth to the old brick palaces and porticoed squares. Previously, it was best known for food – undeniably the richest in the country – and, of course, for its politics. 'Red Bologna' had been the former Italian Left's stronghold and spiritual home since the last war, and it was no coincidence that Bologna's train station was singled out by fascist groups in 1980 for a bomb attack in Italy's worst postwar terrorist atrocity.

After Venice, the city is among the best looking in the country. The city centre is startlingly medieval in plan, a jumble of red brick, tiled roofs and balconies radiating out from the great central square of Piazza Maggiore. There are enough monuments and curiosities for several days' leisured exploration, but Bologna is really enjoyable just for itself, its university and enlightened local government ensuring that there's always something happening – be it theatre, music, the city's strong summer festival, or just the café and bar scene, which is among Italy's most convivial. The only problem is expense: Bologna's latter-day affluence is reflected in a cost of living that is among Italy's highest, exceeding even Florence or Milan; nightlife, particularly, can leave your wallet steam-rolled, and finding a low-priced place to stay can be very difficult.

Bologna's city centre is quite compact, with most things of interest within the main ring road. From the train station, Via dell' Indipendenza leads into the centre; it is one of Bologna's main thoroughfares, lined with cinemas and bars and always busy, finishing up at the linked central squares of Piazza Maggiore and Piazza del Nettuno. To the right of here lies the commercial district, bordered by office blocks along Via g. Marconi, and to the left the university quarter. The one thing you will notice quickly is how well preserved the central area actually is, and although this can be frustrating, too – it's not unusual to find notices on churches suggesting you return in a year's time – the reward is a city centre that is a joy to stroll through. Above all you'll notice the city's famous porticoes – ochre-coloured, vaulted colonnades lining every street into the city centre that make a vivid first impression, especially at night, and that by day provide an unofficial catwalk for Bologna's well turned-out residents.

(Extract from *The Rough Guide to Italy*, Rough Guides)

Using the information in these two articles, produce an account of the reasons for and against visiting Bologna.

You should comment on:

■ things worth seeing and doing;
■ the mood and atmosphere of the city;
■ any disadvantages in going there;
■ how attractive these writers make the place seem.

You should assume that your stay would be only for a couple of days and that everything you are told in the articles is factually correct.

Learning about language: *more about verbs*

In previous units, various forms of verbs have been used, but some have not been named. You need to recognise these names associated with verb forms.

■ **Finite verbs** are verbs which are 'finished', i.e. complete by themselves with their own subject.

For example: The elephant sat in the corner of its cage.
('Sat' is complete in itself, and has its own subject, 'the elephant'.)

■ **Non-finite verbs** are not 'complete' by themselves and do not have a subject. They are usually **infinitives** or **participles**.

■ **The infinitive is the stem form of the verb, with 'to' before it.**

For example: 'to work' is the **present infinitive** (the present tense), of the verb 'work'. The **past infinitive** is 'to have worked'. The **future infinitive** is 'to be about to (or going to) work'.

■ **Verbs have two participles, the present ending in '-ing' and the past ending in '-ed' for regular verbs.**

For example: 'working' and 'worked'.

So far verbs have been classified as regular or irregular according to whether they 'obey the rules' in forming their past tenses. Verbs may also be classified as **transitive** and **intransitive**.

■ **Transitive verbs have a direct object – i.e. something that is affected by the action; intransitive verbs do not.**

For example: In the sentence 'John disliked cigarettes', the direct object – 'cigarettes' – are the objects of John's dislike. 'Dislike' is therefore a **transitive verb**.

In the sentence 'John sleeps soundly', there is no object affected by the action of 'sleeping', so the verb 'sleep' is **intransitive**.

Skills practice: *identifying verb forms*

Exercise A
Read through these ten sentences and then copy out and complete the table, putting a tick in each column if you can find the appropriate verb form in each sentence. Look at this example:

Singing (present participle) *at the top of her voice, Jan* ***rushed*** *(finite verb) up the stairs to her room and started* ***to write*** *(present infinitive) the letter.*

1 Shattered by the missed penalty, Gary sank to his knees.

2 I love to walk along the sand in the moonlight.

3 Screaming hysterically and jumping away from the cupboard, Ben pointed at the mouse that was scampering along the top shelf.

4 Alex was absent all week, struck down by flu.

5 Bitterly disappointed by their visit to the museum, the pupils decided to leave early.

6 Andrew explained how to put on the parachute.

7 Laughing and joking, a couple of passers-by helped us to push the car.

8 Battered but not broken, the soldiers trooped off the field of battle, clutching the remains of their tattered flag.

9 Taking off our shoes, we crept silently along the hall.

10 I love to go climbing in the mountains.

Sentence	Finite verb?	Infinitive?	Present participle?	Past participle?
Example	✓	✓	✓	
1				
2				
3				
4				
5				
6				
7				
8				
9				
10				

Exercise B

Copy out these sentences, highlighting or underlining the transitive and intransitive verbs in different colours.

1 I had been waiting for nearly 30 minutes.

2 The long days of summer were over and the trees were changing from green to gold.

3 The train lay on its side where it had run off the rails.

4 We hammered the nails into the wood with ruthless efficiency.

5 Lisa accepted the present gratefully.

6 The yells from the cellar were becoming louder and louder.

7 My cousin threw the ball straight into the pond.

8 You told me about your accident yesterday.

9 The van mounted the kerb, hit the gatepost and stopped.

10 Siobhan chased Kevin out of the house with a broom.

ord building: *spelling rules: doubling consonants*

These rules apply to most situations when you are adding a suffix to a word stem, whether the suffixes are verb endings, or endings to form nouns, adjectives and adverbs.

The rules are fairly complicated and can be difficult to learn. They are best explained with these examples, and there are more examples for you to practise with.

The best advice is to keep checking back to these rules whenever you need to.

■ **Rule 1: Words of one syllable that end with a consonant after a single vowel, double the consonant before an ending beginning with a vowel.**

For example: drop/dropped
('drop' is a single syllable word ending with a consonant 'p' after a single vowel 'o'. The ending to be added begins with a vowel 'e', so the consonant at the end of the stem – 'p' – is doubled.)

ship/shipping   beg/beggar
lug/luggage   slam/slammed

■ **Rule 2: Words of more than one syllable follow the last rule if they are pronounced with an accent on the final syllable.**

For example: forgot/forgotten
(The emphasis in the two-syllable word 'forgot' falls on the final syllable 'got', so Rule 1 applies.)

But: differ/difference
(The emphasis in the two-syllable word 'differ' falls on the first syllable 'dif', so Rule 1 does not apply and the final consonant is *not* doubled.)

permit/permitted   *but* enter/entering

■ **Rule 3: Words that end in two consonants or a consonant preceded by two vowels do not double the final consonant when adding a suffix.**

For example: part/parted
('part' ends with two consonants, 'rt', so does not double the final consonant 't' when adding a suffix.)
weep/weeping
('weep' ends with a single consonant, 'p', but this follows two vowels, 'ee', so does not double the final consonant 'p' when adding a suffix.)
gold/golden   wait/waiter

■ **Rule 4: Words of more than one syllable that end in 'l' preceded by a single vowel, double the 'l' before an ending beginning with a vowel.**

For example: cancel/cancelled
('Cancel' is a word of two syllables ending with an 'l' preceded by a single vowel 'e'. The ending '-ed' begins with a vowel, 'e', so the final 'l' is doubled.)
appeal/appealing
('Appeal' is a word of two syllables ending with an 'l' preceded by more than one vowel, '-ea'. Although the ending '-ing' begins with a vowel, 'i', the final 'l' is not doubled.)
fulfil/fulfilment   steal/stealing

Skills practice: *doubling consonants*

Exercise A
Complete these words with the correct spelling, using Rule 1.
The first one has been done for you.

big + –er	*bigger*
win + –er	
run + –ing	
whip + –ed	
rid + –ance	
step + –ing	
wet + –est	
shrug + –ed	
nag + –ing	
rob + –er	
sit + –ing	

continued …

Exercise B

Complete these words with the correct spelling, using Rule 2.
The first one has been done for you.

woman + –ish	*womanish*
loyal + –ist	
regret + –able	
begin + –ing	
offer + –ed	
consider + –ing	
upset + –ing	
happen + –ed	
murder + –er	
prosper + –ous	
visit + –or	

Exercise C

Complete these words with the correct spelling, using Rule 3.
The first one has been done for you.

sweet + –en	*sweeten*
seat + –ed	
rip + –ing	
cheap + –en	
rot + –en	
sweat + –er	
long + –est	
read + –ing	
fall + –ing	
fast + –er	
thin + –est	

Exercise D

Complete these words with the correct spelling, using Rule 4.
The first one has been done for you.

repeal + –ed	*repealed*
appal + –ing	
fulfil + –ed	
pedal + –ed	
jewel + –er	
rebel + –ious	
tunnel + –ed	
travel + –er	
rail + –ing	
fail + –ure	
marvel + –ous	

Text building: *using commas*

In Unit 2, you learned about using commas to separate items in a list.

■ Commas are also used to break up complex sentences.

■ You need to use them as you become better at building sentences using phrases and subordinate clauses.

■ **Rule 1: When a subordinate clause comes before a main clause, it is separated off by a comma.**

For example: When you are ready, we shall leave.
            If you don't understand, ask me for help.

■ **Rule 2: Commas are used to separate off a non-defining subordinate clause from the rest of the sentence.**

(Note: a defining clause is one that is so closely related to the person or object that it defines, that the meaning would not be clear without this clause.)

For example: This is the house *we live in*.
            (defining clause – no comma!)

My sister Karen, *who is a staff nurse*, is getting married in the spring.
(non-defining clause – use commas!)

■ **Rule 3: Commas are used to separate off adjectival/ participle phrases.**

For example: The speaker, *getting to his feet*, knocked over a glass of water. (adjectival/participle phrase)

■ **Rule 4: Commas are used to separate off phrases in apposition, that is, phrases that give an alternative description of something or someone.**

For example: Mrs Carter, *my next-door neighbour*, went on holiday to Tunisia. (phrase in apposition)

■ **Rule 5: Commas are usually used to separate off the following words from the rest of the sentence: too, however, nevertheless, though, of course.**

For example: We, however, have never made that mistake. You, of course, are unlikely to achieve so much again.

Skills practice: *using commas*

Exercise A
Copy out these sentences and add commas, following Rules 1 and 2.

1 He was riding a bicycle which was remarkable considering his age.
2 When you see him give him my love.
3 Although I was tired I didn't go to bed.
4 These are the scissors that I use for cutting flowers.
5 This is something we try not to talk about.
6 My cousin Jason who is a fantastic footballer is coming to stay for a month.
7 I shall wait as long as necessary.
8 Mr Evans will punish her if she speaks again.
9 You should have seen the mess after the party was over.
10 There's a river at the end of the garden where we can go for a swim.

Exercise B

Copy out these sentences and add commas, following Rules 3, 4 and 5.

1 The game being over all the spectators went home.

2 The table made of mahogany was Mum's favourite wedding present.

3 They all nevertheless agreed to his suggestion.

4 The engine once stopped was difficult to start again.

5 John refused and whether you believe it or not so did his sister.

6 Robert the youngest of the family went off to London.

7 You must of course ask your parents' permission before you come on the trip.

8 This bread untouched by hand throughout the whole manufacturing process is no more expensive than that.

9 I however have never seen him at all.

10 This as you can see is the last one.

Writing

- Using the notes from your group work at the start of this unit, prepare an article for your local newspaper giving the attractions of a weekend break in your area.

- Give details of 5–10 places worth visiting, including any special attractions.

- Aim your feature at young people if you wish.

LOCAL NEWS WEEKLY

Out and about in N

ICT Extra!

Creating your own website
Check out any websites for towns and other places of interest in your area. Adapt your piece of writing, supported by whatever pictures, photographs and other presentational (DTP) means you have, to create a website for your chosen place.

Unit 11: Drop that 'e'!

In this unit you will:

- read an extract from a play;
- learn more verbs;
- learn about and practise spelling rules;
- learn about and practise the use of semi-colons and colons.

Speaking and listening

- Work in groups of three for this role play.

- One person takes the part of a pupil on a school trip who has misbehaved. You will need to work out what has happened. The other two are teachers.

- The teachers begin by interviewing the trouble-maker to discover the facts, then have a discussion about what action to take. One should take a more severe line than the other.

- At the end of the role play, the 'troublesome pupil' should explain to the two teachers how fair he or she thinks their treatment and the decisions taken have been.

- Begin 'out of role', by jotting down a few ideas and an outline situation.

Understanding

Playwrights have to use dialogue to convey what their characters are like and to give actors some idea on how the characters might behave. Characters can be studied from the 'outside' by looking carefully at what they do and say. You can track their progress and function throughout the whole play, noting their interactions with other characters. But characters may also be studied from the 'inside', by 'getting inside the skin' of a particular character and viewing events and the behaviour of the other characters through that one person's eyes.

Read this extract from Willy Russell's play *Our Day Out*. In order to complete the task that follows, you will need to 'get inside' the characters of the two teachers, Mrs Kay and Mr Briggs.

A group of special needs pupils from a school on Merseyside have been taken out on a day trip to the North Wales coast; for many of them, a rare treat. Mrs Kay is the special needs teacher who has organised the trip; Mr Briggs has been sent along by the head teacher to 'keep an eye on things'. Carol and Andrews are two pupils.

Our Day Out

Carol is sitting on the battlements, looking out over the estuary.
Nearby, on a bench, Mrs Kay is sitting back enjoying the sun.

Mrs Kay   Why don't you go and have a look around the castle, Carol? You haven't seen it yet.

5 **Carol**   Miss, I don't like it. It's horrible. I'd rather sit here with you an' look at the lake.

Mrs Kay   That's the sea.

Carol   Yeh, that's what I mean.

Andrews (*runs on and joins them*)   Miss, miss, I just thought of this
10 great idea; miss, wouldn't it be smart if we had somethin' like this castle round our way. The kids wouldn't get into trouble, would they, if they had somewhere like this to play.

Carol   Miss, we couldn't have somethin' like this round our way, could we?

15 **Mrs Kay**   Why not?

Carol   'Cos if we had somethin' like this we'd only wreck it, wouldn't we?

Andrews   No we wouldn't.

continued …

Carol We would. That's why we never have nothin' nice

20 round our way – we'd smash it up. The corporation knows that
an' so why should they waste their time and money. They'd give
us nice things if we looked after them, but we don't, do we?

Andrews Miss, d' y' know what I think about it, miss?

Mrs Kay Go on John, what?

25 **Andrews** Miss, miss, if all this belonged to us – like it wasn't
the corporation's but it was something that we owned, well we
wouldn't let no one wreck it, would we? Eh? We'd look after it,
wouldn't we? Defend it. D'y' know what I mean, miss?

Mrs Kay Yes, I think I do. *(Briggs enters.)* What you're saying …

30 **Briggs** Right. You two, off. Go on, move.

Carol Sir, where?

Briggs Anywhere girl. Just move. I want to talk to Mrs Kay.
Well come on then.

*The two **kids** reluctantly wander off. **Briggs** waits until they are out*

35 *of hearing.*

Mrs Kay *(quietly angry)* I was talking to those children.

Briggs Yes, an' I'm talking to you, Mrs Kay. This has got to stop.

Mrs Kay Pardon me. What's got to stop?

Briggs What! Can't you see what's going on? It's a shambles,

40 the whole ill-organised affair. Just look what they did at the zoo.
Look. *(As a group of **kids** run past playing chase and tick.)* They're
just left to race and chase and play havoc. God knows what the
castle authorities must think. Now look, when you bring
children like this into this sort of environment you can't afford

45 to just let them roam free.

Kids rushing past.

Briggs They're just like town dogs let off the leash in the
country. My God, for some of them it's the first time they've
been further than Birkenhead.

50 **Mrs Kay** *(quietly)* I know. And I was just thinking: it's a shame
really, isn't it? We bring them out to a crumbling pile of bricks
and mortar and they think they're in the fields of heaven.

Briggs   You *are* on their side aren't you?

Mrs Kay   Absolutely Mr Briggs, absolutely.

55 *A couple of **kids** shouting to try and hear the echo of their names.*

Briggs   Look, all I want to know from you is what you're going to do about this chaos?

Mrs Kay   Well I'd suggest that if you want the chaos to stop you should simply look at it not as chaos but what it actually

60 is – kids, with a bit of space around them, making a bit of noise. All right, so the head asked you to come along – but can't you just relax? There's no point in pretending that a day out to Wales is going to be of some great educational benefit to them. It's too late for them. Most of these kids were rejects the

65 day they came into the world. We're not going to solve anything today, Mr Briggs. Can't we just give them a good day out? Mm? At least we could try and do that.

Briggs   Well, that's a fine attitude, isn't it? That's a fine attitude for a member of the teaching profession.

70 **Mrs Kay** (*beginning to let her temper go*)   Well, what's your alternative? Eh? Pretending? Pretending that they've got some sort of a future ahead of them? Even if you cared for these kids you couldn't help to make a future for them. You won't educate them because nobody wants them educating.

75 **Briggs**   Listen, Mrs Kay …

Mrs Kay   No you listen, Mr Briggs, you listen and perhaps you'll stop fooling yourself. Teach them? Teach them what? You'll never teach them because nobody knows what to do with them. Ten years ago you could teach them to stand in a line, you could teach

80 them to obey, to expect little more than a lousy factory job. But now they haven't even got that to aim for. Mr Briggs, you won't teach them because you're in a job that's designed and funded to fail! There's nothing for them to do, any of them; most of them were born for factory fodder, but the factories have closed down.

85 **Briggs**   And I suppose that's the sort of stuff you've been pumping into their minds.

> **Mrs Kay** *(laughing)*   And you really think they'd understand?
>
> **Briggs**   I'm not going to spend any more time arguing with you. You may have organised this visit, but I'm the one who
> 90 was sent by the headmaster to supervise. Now, either you take control of the children in your charge or I'll be forced to abandon this visit and order everyone home.
>
> **Mrs Kay**   Well ... that's your decision. But I'm not going to let you prevent the kids from having some fun. If you want to
> 95 abandon this visit you'd better start walking because we're not going home. We're going down to the beach!

Now give a full and detailed account of how Willy Russell reveals the different attitudes of Mrs Kay and Mr Briggs.

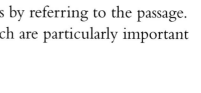

You should comment on:

■ how they each speak to and treat the pupils;

■ the way they talk about the pupils, especially the words they use;

■ the way they talk about their job as teachers;

■ how far you think each of them is a good teacher.

Remember to support your opinions by referring to the passage. Quote actual words and phrases which are particularly important to your point of view.

Learning about language: *auxiliary and modal verbs*

In previous units various forms of verbs have been used. In some cases finite forms of verbs have been combined with parts of other verbs to make a **verb phrase**.

For example: ■ finite forms of the verb to be – 'is', 'was', etc. – are used to create the continuous form of the present or past tense.

- finite forms of the verb 'do' are used to create emphatic forms of verbs.
- 'will' and 'shall' are used to create future tense forms.
- finite forms of the verb 'have' are used to create past tense forms.

(In Unit 12, you will discover how the creation of **conditional forms** involve the use of 'should' and 'would'.)

When these verbs are used in this way, they are called **auxiliary verbs** ('auxiliary' means additional, giving help, giving support). They help create the appropriate verb form.

There is another group of verbs, sometimes used as auxiliaries, called modal verbs. The most common forms of these verbs are:

- can
- may
- must/have to
- ought
- used to.

Sometimes these verbs are not used clearly and accurately.

- **'can' (past form 'could') is used to express 'being able to' or 'being possible to'**

  For example: You can do it when you try! (i.e. you have the necessary ability)

  You can ski today. (i.e. there is enough snow)

  I could run a mile in ten minutes when I was younger.

- **'may' is used to express permission ('being allowed to') or speculation ('it's possible that')**

  For example: You may go to the disco because your mother has agreed. (i.e. have permission)

  (For actions in the past, the verb 'allow' is used: You were allowed to go to the disco as a reward for all that hard work.)

I may go to the disco tomorrow if I feel like it.
(i.e. it's a possibility)

(For actions in the past, the verb 'may' is used with 'have' plus the past participle of the verb: I may have caught it last week on holiday.)

■ **'must'/'have to' is used to express something that is 'really essential'**

For example: He must work harder if he is to pass his exams.
(i.e. it is absolutely essential)

(For actions in the past, 'must have' plus the past participle of the verb or 'had to' plus the infinitive are used: He must have worked/had to work very long hours to earn all that money.)

■ **'ought to'/'should' are used to express some degree of obligation or duty, or to give advice**

For example: You should/ought to finish your homework before going out. (i.e. if you were a good student!)

You should/ought to finish your homework if you don't want to get into trouble. (i.e. remember school rules about homework!)

(For actions in the past, 'should'/'ought to' are used with 'have' plus the past participle of the verb: You should have done your homework last night.)

■ **'used (to)' is the past form of a verb that has no present tense. It is used to express a discontinued habit or a past routine (possibly still carried on)**

For example: I used to play basketball on Tuesdays.

Skills practice: *using auxiliary verbs*

Exercise A

Copy out these sentences, completing the verb phrases with the appropriate form of an auxiliary verb. Look at the example.

> Phoebe **does** not seem very interested in history, but you **have** always worked hard in this subject.

1 I _____ feeling happy today because I _____ celebrating my birthday.

2 The Prime Minister _____ to make a statement this evening.

3 Two of his teeth _____ knocked out in the fight.

4 Why _____ you wear glasses?

5 She _____ worn glasses since she was a child because she _____ very short-sighted.

6 He _____ seen that film six times if he _____ going to see it again tomorrow.

7 I know that you _____ not expect me to go but in the end I _____.

8 We _____ our windows cleaned every month.

9 That animal _____ eaten so much, it can't drag itself to its feet!

10 I _____ buy a new pen for the exams.

Exercise B

Copy out these sentences, completing the verb phrases with the appropriate form of one of the modal verbs: can, may, must/ have to/ought, used to. Look at the example.

You **must** clean your boots; you **may** not go out with them in that state.

1 You will _____ clean your boots when you join the army.

2 You _____ leave early tomorrow.

3 _____ you speak French?

4 We _____ be able to swim here, but now it's too dangerous.

5 I _____ have returned my library books last week.

6 You _____ be at school early for tomorrow's trip.

7 Young people _____ not smoke so much because it damages their health.

8 She _____ sit at the back of the class and never say anything.

9 Mr Wilkinson _____ not know that you are here.

10 Will _____ drive quite well although he still hasn't passed his test.

Word building: *spelling rules: the silent '-e'*

■ **Words ending with a silent '-e', that is an 'e' that follows a consonant, drop the '-e' before a suffix beginning with a vowel.**

For example: 'love' forms 'loving', 'loved' and 'lovable' by dropping the final, silent 'e', because '-ing', '-ed' and '-able' are all suffixes beginning with a vowel.

But 'love' forms 'lovely', keeping the final 'e', because '-ly' is a suffix that begins with a consonant.

Exceptions:

■ **Words ending in '-ce' and '-ge' keep the final 'e' before a suffix beginning with '-a', '-o' or '-u'.**

For example: 'manage' forms 'managing' but 'manageable'

■ **Words ending in '-ce', change the 'e' to 'i' before the suffix '-ous'**

For example: 'grace' forms 'gracious', changing the 'e' to 'i'.

■ **Words ending in '-able'/'-ible' drop the final 'e' when adding the suffix '-ly'.**

For example: 'comfortable' forms 'comfortably'
'incredible' forms 'incredibly'

■ **The final '-e' is also dropped in the following words:**

true – truly;   due – duly;   whole – wholly

Note: the rule applies to words ending with a silent '-e' after a consonant; words ending in '-ee' do not drop an 'e' before a vowel suffix.

For example: 'agree' forms 'agreed'; 'foresee' forms 'foreseeable'.

Skills practice: *the silent –e*

Exercise A
Complete this table by adding the endings indicated to the words given. The first one has been done for you as an example.

Stem + suffix	Correct form
write + –er	*writer*
wise + –ly	
tire + –some	
use + –ful	
noise + –y	
pleasure + –able	
move + –ment	
hope + –less	
compose + –ed	
arrive + –ing	
dispose + –able	

(Note: watch the spelling of some of these!)

Exercise B
Complete this table by adding the suffixes indicated to these words ending in –ce or –ge. The first one has been done for you as an example.

Stem + suffix	Correct form
advantage + –ous	*advantageous*
spice + –y	
age + –less	
service + –able	
space + –ous	
enlarge + –ment	
trace + –ing	
knowledge + –able	
arrange + –ed	
peace + –ful	
malice + –ous	

(Note: watch the spelling of some of these!)

Text building: *using semi-colons and colons*

- **The semi-colon is used to separate statements which are separate yet so closely connected that a full stop would be too complete a break.**

  It is a lesser stop than a full stop; it is a sort of halfway house between a comma and a full stop. The statements it separates may themselves be complete sentences.

  For example: The first thing she bought was a new dress; the last thing was a new hat.

- **The semi-colon is also used to separate items in a list, when the items are phrases or clauses rather than individual words. (You can also use a comma in this way; see Unit 10.)**

  For example: As we set off on the picnic, Dad carried the rugs; Mum had the food; Lesley was struggling with two chairs; and I carried everything else!

- **The colon is used to introduce a list, an example or an explanation or reason.**

  For example: These are the things we shall need for the picnic: rugs, a flask of coffee and some sandwiches. (i.e. a list)

  The problem is this: which came first, the chicken or the egg? (i.e. an explanation)

  There are many things people look for in a good holiday: plenty to do, perhaps. (i.e. an example)

Skills practice: *using semi-colons and colons*

Copy out these sentences, adding semi-colons and colons where necessary.

1 Firstly, you should listen carefully then you should write down what you hear.

2 It was lucky for us we had our coats lucky as well that we hadn't gone far.

3 The traffic light rules are very simple if the light is red, you stop if green, you go if amber, you wait.

4 Put all the books you have in the spare room the novels, the plays and the poetry.

5 All I need is this someone who can answer the telephone and take messages.

6 The house was derelict it had stood empty for over ten years.

7 Solving this mystery is easy find the woman.

8 You should always consult a good dictionary the Oxford or Collins.

9 He frequently had backache so frequently he was always visiting the doctor.

10 They came they looked over the house they didn't buy it.

Writing

- Return to your role play at the start of this unit. Build a short play around the ideas that were created in the role play.

- You may change or add to the characters, but try to make some sort of difference of opinion the central point of your play.

- What caused the problem? Why did the characters have different opinions about it? How were things finally sorted out?

- Remember to make the dialogue – the words the characters actually say – reflect the differences in their personalities and points of view.

- Set out your play in the usual way, with the name of the character speaking before each speech, the stage directions in brackets, etc. Look back at the extract from *Our Day Out* at the beginning of the unit to see how it is set out.

- Although you are writing 'spoken English', remember the rules of spelling and sentence punctuation you have been learning and practising.

Unit 12: Moody verbs

In this unit you will:

- read a short report on the need for a world language;
- learn about the 'mood' and 'voice' of verbs;
- learn to check words that are easily confused;
- learn about and practise the use of conditional clauses.

Speaking and listening

- Work in groups of about five.
- It has been decided to set aside some money for a project to commemorate the fiftieth anniversary of the founding of your school. Decide what this project should be. Your choice should benefit future members of the school and possibly the community; it should not just be a static display.
- Think about costs and raising additional money if necessary. Choose someone to act as chairman of your group – 'to keep order' – and someone else to write notes of all the decisions your group makes.
- At the end of the task, each group chairman should give a brief report to the whole class.

Understanding

Impersonal writing, by its very definition, attempts to leave out the personality, opinions and beliefs of the writer in order to emphasise facts and evidence. It attempts to be objective rather than personal, offering cold, factual and sensible explanations, free of prejudice and independent of judgement. It might be used for accounts of scientific experiments and other sorts of unbiased investigations. Its objectivity can make it sound very persuasive when developing an argument for a certain line of action.

Read this report on the need for a 'world language' which all nations could use and which might improve international understanding and communication. Then answer the questions that follow.

A World Language

The creation of a common European currency unit may represent a small step towards greater economic co-operation between nations, but the real communications problem lies in the 3,000
5 different languages and dialects spoken throughout the world. This did not matter in past centuries when communications between different parts of the world were slow and difficult and when, in Europe at least, all educated men spoke Latin.

10   However, things have changed completely in our century. While few people can speak Latin, telecommunications technology has made it possible to talk directly between continents. Modern forms of transport mean that a journey which might have taken several weary weeks can now be achieved in a few
15 hours. As a result, it's hardly surprising that many people have felt an increasing need for a common language, and on a number of occasions throughout the last century various solutions to the problem have been put forward.

20   The first of these was the creation of a completely artificial tongue, quite unconnected with any existing language. Although such a tongue might be difficult for people to learn, it at least had the advantage that everyone started on an equal footing.

A second suggested solution was the invention of
25 a synthetic language based on natural languages, but without their numerous irregularities. Esperanto is the best known language in this category and, since such a language would be related to existing languages, it would be easier to
30 learn, at least for European speakers, although less accessible to the world-wide community.

Two other solutions to the problem of an international language are: either to adopt some existing language already spoken by a large
35 number of people or nations (such languages as French, Spanish or Russian might be suitable); or to take one of these languages and create a simplified version, in which the vocabulary and grammatical forms would be reduced to a minimum.

40   In the end, it seems unlikely that the governments of the world will ever formally agree on an international language, but meanwhile, whether we like it or not, there are increasing signs that English is becoming accepted as a second language by a majority of people all over
45 the world.

Now answer these questions:

1 What is the 'communications problem' that has arisen as a result of technological changes in recent decades?

2 What are the advantages and disadvantages of the first two solutions suggested?

3 What are the advantages of the two further solutions put forward?

4 How, in the writer's opinion, will the problem be solved?

5 Look back through this short report and explain how it is presented in a way that helps the reader to understand the issues and points made.

You should comment on:

- the way ideas are organised;
- the words and phrases that are used to help guide the reader through the article;
- the choice of words, including pronouns;
- the use of verb forms – especially 'voice'.

Learning about language: *the 'mood' and 'voice' of verbs*

You may not very often use some terms that describe the grammatical forms of verbs. However, it is important to recognise these forms and understand what they do and how this affects their meaning.

- **Verbs have four moods: indicative, imperative, interrogative and subjunctive.** These 'moods' occur in all tense forms; they simply show how the verb is being used.

- **The indicative mood is by far the most common. It is the form in which the verb 'indicates' (describes) what's going on (the action).**

For example: The cat is sleeping peacefully on the bed.

We have eaten fish pie for lunch.

■ **The imperative mood is used when a command is given.**

For example: Go away!

Tell Dad to stop snoring!

■ **The interrogative mood is used when a question is asked.**

For example: Have you seen Jackie this morning?

Did you really say that?

■ **The subjunctive mood is far less common. It is used in certain exclamations to express a wish or hope, or after verbs that express wishes, hopes, doubts and similar feelings. It is also used in some conditional sentences which you will learn about later in this unit.**

For example: Heaven be praised!

I wish I were a rich man.

If I had/were to have the money, I wouldn't know what to do with it! ★

★*(Note: this form of the verb has fallen into disuse in modern speech and written English. It is only regularly used in 'If I were you' and 'I wish that were true'.)*

■ **Verbs have two 'voices': the active voice and the passive voice.** These 'voices' occur in all forms of tense and mood; they simply show how the verb is being used. In other words, each verb may have a different mood for each tense and a different voice for each tense and mood. (Work out how many possible combinations of tenses, mood and voice there are, when you have a spare moment!)

■ **The active voice is the commonest form, with a subject performing an action.**

For example: Sally **is writing** her diary.

Pupils usually **understand** the rules of grammar.

■ **The passive voice is used when it is more important to stress the action than the performer of the action. It is, therefore, used to give an impersonal effect, for example in scientific writing or objective reports.**

For example: The jewels **were stolen** from the wall safe.

An electric current **was passed** through the chemicals.

■ **The active form of the verb may be turned into the passive (and vice versa) by rearranging the sentence.**

For example: 'Sally was writing her diary' would become 'The diary was written by Sally.'

'Pupils usually understand the rules of grammar' would become 'The rules of grammar are usually understood by pupils'.

You can see from these examples that changing the 'voice' of the verb changes the pattern of the sentence and gives emphasis to different parts of the sentence.

Skills practice: *recognising the mood and voice of verbs*

Exercise A

Read through these sentences and complete the table, indicating the mood of the verb forms. Look back to the rules on pages 120–122 to help you. The first one has been done for you as an example.

1 Will you be at home this evening?   *interrogative*

2 Other children always say 'Please' and 'Thank you'.   _____

3 Stop running immediately.   _____

4 If I were you, I'd give up now.   _____

5 The ball crashed into the boundary fence.   _____

6 Are you cooking pizza for supper?   _____

7 Heaven help us!   _____

8 Wait there until I tell you.   _____

9 I wish I were playing for England.   _____

10 The new naval recruits went to sea.   _____

Exercise B

Re-shape these sentences into the opposite voice from the present one, i.e. turn the active into passive and vice versa. Look at the examples again, before you do the exercise.

You should have checked this exercise before handing it in.
This exercise should have been checked before it was handed in.

1 No one has climbed this mountain before.

2 He has not been seen since yesterday.

3 Mr Edwards was given a leaving present by all his colleagues on his retirement.

4 The school choir sang excerpts from *Jesus Christ Superstar* at the concert.

5 No one has tuned this piano in years.

6 Pupils distributed gifts to senior citizens after their harvest festival.

7 You are not allowed to smoke in any part of the building.

8 When Mrs Evans marked my book, she proved all my calculations were wrong.

9 Many road accidents are caused by drinking and driving.

10 In 1966 England beat West Germany in the World Cup Final.

Word building: *words that are easily confused*

It is easy to confuse words that sound the same or look similar, especially if you are writing at speed. Words that sound the same are called 'homophones'. Many are the little words that are used frequently, so it's important to be aware of their different forms and check for these mistakes when you have finished a first draft of a piece of writing.

- **there; their; they're**

    There refers to a place (like 'here'), or is used with verbs to express a general point.

    For example: I left it there yesterday. (i.e. at that place)

    There is too much noise in this classroom. (i.e. no particular individual mentioned)

    There are two wasps buzzing about behind your head. (i.e. a generalised statement, even though 'you' are involved)

    Their means 'belonging to them'.

    For example: Their dog is in our garden again. (i.e. 'they' own the dog)

    They have to change buses twice when making their way home from school. (i.e. the journey 'belongs to' them; other people have other journeys!)

    They're is the shortened form of 'they are', often used when writing direct speech.

    For example: They're only looking for attention! (i.e. 'they're' could be replaced by the full form 'they are')

    Now it's broken, they're going to be in trouble with the head teacher.

- **its; it's**

    Its – without the apostrophe – means 'belonging to it'.

    For example: The elephant lifted up its trunk and took the bun. (i.e. the trunk belonging to the elephant)

It's – with the apostrophe – is the shortened form of 'it is' or 'it has'.

For example: It's been a wonderful day. (i.e. 'it has been')

It's a long time to spend in an aeroplane for just a few hours away. (i.e. 'it is a long time …')

■ **your; you're**

Your means 'belonging to you'.

For example: Your hamster has got out of its cage. (i.e. the hamster which belongs to you)

You're is the shortened form of 'you are'.

For example: You're late! (i.e. 'you are late')

■ **two; to; too**

Two is always used for the number 2.

For example: I bought a new pencil, a pen and two refills. (i.e. 'two' answers the question 'how many?')

To is used to form the infinitive of a verb (see Unit 10) and to show direction towards something, someone or somewhere.

For example: I want you to work on your skills in this area. (i.e. forms the infinitive of 'work')

The family went on holiday to Spain in the summer. (i.e. idea of 'towards' a place)

Too has just two meanings – 'also' and 'very'.

For example: We are going on holiday too. (i.e. 'also' or 'as well')

It's too cold to go swimming this morning. (i.e. 'very cold' or 'excessively cold')

■ **of; off**

(These words are not homophones, so the way they are pronounced should help you distinguish between them.)

Of is most commonly used to mean 'belonging to' or 'created/composed from'.

For example: The last days of the summer holiday were wet and cold. (i.e. 'belonging to')

The door was made of chipwood and plasterboard. (i.e. 'built from')

Off most commonly expresses ideas of 'away from' or 'separation'.

For example: You get off the bus opposite the hospital. (i.e. 'separation')

They have gone off on holiday without cancelling the milk. (i.e. 'away from')

■ **past; passed**

Past is used to mean 'by' or 'beyond', of both time and place.

For example: It's well past your bedtime. (i.e. it's 'beyond' your bedtime)

The number 63 bus goes past your school. (i.e. goes 'by' or 'beyond' your school)

Past generations gave their lives in the service of their country. (i.e. generations 'gone by' or 'beyond recall')

Passed is the past tense form of the verb 'pass'. It may therefore be preceded by 'I', 'she', 'they' etc., because it describes an action.

For example: He passed his exam with flying colours.

Gemma passed the information on to her teacher.

*(Note: 'You went **past** it on your way to school,' but 'You **passed** it on your way to school', because 'past' cannot be used as a verb.)*

Skills practice: *words that are easily confused*

Exercise A
Complete the sentences on page 127 with the correct word chosen from:

there, their, they're
its, it's
of, off.

Look at the following example:

What kind **of** dog is it?

1 Why aren't _____ chips for tea?

2 Get your hand _____ my arm!

3 _____ are 18 shopping days left until Christmas.

4 What sort _____ present do you want?

5 The children were doing _____ end _____ term exams.

6 The cat seems to have hurt _____ paw.

7 Look at those idiots; _____ laughing _____ heads off!

8 _____ very cold for this time of year.

9 _____ toes and fingers were absolutely frozen.

10 The water was turned _____ regularly during the drought.

Exercise B

Complete these sentences with the correct word chosen from:

two, to, too
your, you're
past, passed.

Look at the following example:

We're going **to** the disco on Saturday.

1 I'm _____ tired _____ do my homework.

2 It's half _____ eight already and _____ breakfast is waiting.

3 There were only _____ sweets left in the bag.

4 I _____ my sweets round, but David didn't!

5 The teachers seemed _____ be enjoying the party _____ .

6 _____ going to be in trouble now!

7 The train _____ through Doncaster on its way to York.

8 _____ bedroom is a total disgrace, it's so untidy!

9 He realised he was _____ late as the bus sped _____ the stop while he was still _____ fifty metres away.

10 Make up _____ own mind.

Text building: *using conditional forms*

An action often depends on a **condition**, that is, another action introduced by the word 'if'. In these sentences, it is very easy to make mistakes matching up the correct tense forms of the verbs.

Conditional sentences may be divided into three groups:
- **Group 1: Sentences that express cause and effect. The verb in the 'if' clause is in the present or future tense; the verb in the main clause is also in the present or future tense.**

> (a) If you buy (present tense) a car, it costs (present) a lot of money.
>
> (b) If you buy that car (present), it will cost (future) you a lot of money.
>
> (c) If you should buy a car (future), it will cost (future) you a lot of money.

- **Group 2: Sentences that express hypothetical (possible) situations that are not resolved.**
  The verb in the 'if' clause is in the past tense; the verb in the main clause is in the conditional – 'would' – form.
  (The simple past tense has actually replaced a subjunctive form 'If I were to …')

> (a) If I dropped (were to drop) this, it would explode.
> (I could drop this, then everything would be resolved. At this stage things are still not certain.)
>
> (b) If you bought (were to buy) a car, it would cost a lot of money.

- **Group 3: Sentences that express hypothetical (possible) situations that are resolved.**
  The verb in the 'if' clause is in the 'distant' past (or past perfect) – 'had' – tense; the verb in the main clause is in the past conditional – 'would have' – form.

> (a) If he had known of her arrival, he would have met her. (But he didn't know, so he didn't meet her. The situation is resolved; it cannot be altered.)
>
> (b) If you had bought a car last year, it would have cost you a lot of money.

■ Whenever you use an 'if' (conditional) clause, check back to this section to make sure you have the correct sequence of tense forms.

■ Keep checking back until you are confident you have mastered the rules.

Skills practice: *using conditionals*

Exercise A
Copy out these sentences and complete them with the correct form of the verb given in brackets, applying the rules for 'Group 1' conditionals.
1 If you say that again, I (hit) you.
2 If the train is late, it (delay) the start of the competition.
3 If I don't find my glasses soon, I (have) a headache.
4 If they (arrive) early, they will stay at the station until we get there.
5 If you (throw) a stone into the pond, it will sink.
6 If she takes away his toys, he (cry).
7 If you move a muscle, I (hit) you.
8 If you (decide) to tell me, it will save a lot of time.
9 If we hang out with people like that, we (get) into trouble.
10 If they (listen) to me carefully, I will explain.

Exercise B
Copy out these sentences and complete them with the correct form of the verb given in brackets, applying the rules for 'Group 2' conditionals.
1 If his grandmother ever met her, she (be) delighted.
2 If they played together regularly, they (win) more often.
3 If that lorry (go) over the old bridge, the bridge would collapse.
4 If I had more money, I (wear) more fashionable clothes.
5 If you really wanted to learn the clarinet, I (need) to speak to the Director of Music.
6 If you spoke to her in a pleasant way, she (serve) you more quickly.
7 If it had more seasoning, this soup (taste) much better.
8 If they really (try), they would win first prize easily.
9 If he (be) a gentleman, he would not speak like that.
10 If you took more exercise, you (be) much fitter.

Exercise C

Copy out these sentences and complete them with the correct form of the verb given in brackets, applying the rules for 'Group 3' conditionals.

1 If the removal men had been stronger, they (lift) the wardrobe easily.

2 If I had known the answer, I (tell) you.

3 If she (explain) it properly, I would have understood at once.

4 If we had saved our money when we were younger, we (be) rich by now.

5 If the dog (tie up), it would not have bitten me.

6 If they had travelled by train, they (arrive) by now.

7 If it had not rained, we (play) tennis yesterday.

8 If I had realised she was so busy, I (leave) immediately.

9 If they (know) how, they would have done it themselves.

10 If Usha (eat) all those sweets, she would have been sick.

Writing

■ Return to your school anniversary project.

■ Write a persuasive report for the headteacher of your school, setting out three possible projects. Explain their advantages and disadvantages and how you think additional money might be raised.

■ Refer to the passage you read at the beginning of this unit and think about how your report should be organised and set out, so that your information and opinions are clearly presented.

■ Think about the use of appropriate verb forms, including the passive voice and subjunctive mood (if you use conditional ['if'] clauses). Check back to the examples and practice exercises in this unit to make sure you use these correctly.

■ Complete your report with a firm recommendation on which project should be chosen.

Unit 13: Dash it!

In this unit you will:

- read an extract from *Basketball Game*;
- learn about adverbs and their use;
- learn about and practise forming adverbs;
- learn about and practise using parentheses.

Speaking and listening

- Working with a partner, list at least six sorts of prejudices you hear every day:
  - boys talking about girls and vice versa;
  - pupils from one year group about another;
  - pupils about teachers (and vice versa?!);
  - people with different accents;
  - people who support different football teams, etc.

- Tell each other about a time when you think you were treated unfairly because someone was prejudiced.

- How did you feel? How did you cope with the situation? What do you think now when you look back on it?

- What can be done to stop prejudice?

(Note: be sensitive to other people's feelings as you deal with these issues.)

Understanding

Unit 11 focused on how dialogue may reveal aspects of people's character and beliefs. Often feelings and attitudes are hinted at through particular words and phrases that gradually build up to give a fuller picture of a person's character. Read this extract from *Basketball Game* by Julius Lester. Then answer fully the questions that follow.

The story on the next page is set in the United States of America. Allen is a black teenager who has recently moved house to a new area and wishes to join the local library. (You will notice that some of the spellings, e.g. colored, favorite, are the American forms.)

Allen walked quickly up the steps, studiously ignoring the white faces he passed. He went into the building as if he'd been there many times and walked to the desk. When the old white woman looked up, her jaw dropped. 'What you want?' she said sharply.

5   'I'd like to apply for a library card,' he said firmly.

'You can't come to this library,' she said nervously.

Allen could feel his heart pounding as he noticed the white people in the library gathering a short distance away. He didn't know what to do, but he knew he couldn't walk out of that library
10 past all those white faces. He couldn't let them run him away.

'Why not?' he said calmly.

'You just can't,' the old woman said, more agitated. She had lowered her head and
15 was busy stamping some cards on her desk.

'I would take proper care of the books.' He spoke distinctly and evenly, betraying no
20 emotion and being very careful not to sound colored, like his father. And though he was angry, his voice was as pleasant as if he were talking about the weather.

25   'This is the white library!' the old woman blurted out. 'You people have your own library.'

Allen hadn't known there was a colored library, but it didn't matter. 'But one does not have the wide choice of books there that are available here. And I think it's the duty of all Americans to be
30 as fully educated as they can be. Don't you agree?' He almost burst out laughing and wished his father was there to see him.

The old librarian turned a deep red and refused to answer.

When Allen realized that she was going to ignore him, he
35 became frightened. He couldn't let her win. He simply couldn't. 'Is there a law against my availing myself of these facilities?'

40 'Yes,' the woman snapped.

'Might I see it, please? I'm not familiar with it.'

'Where you from, boy?' the woman asked evenly, looking at him through narrowed eyes. 'You don't talk like you from Nashville.'

45 'No, I'm not. I've just moved to the city from Pine Bluff, Arkansas.' And it wasn't a total lie. He had been in Pine Bluff for a week before they came to Nashville. It was obvious, however, that he wasn't going to get a library card. He could sense that a crowd had gathered, and he knew that if he continued to press her
50 something might happen. He didn't know what – she might call the police. But he had to have a library card.

Just then a young white woman came out of a back office. Uh-oh, he thought. The old woman had probably pushed a buzzer under her desk, or somebody went and got this younger one and
55 she was coming out to tell him to leave before she called the cops.

'May I help you?' the woman said pleasantly.

'Yes, I would like to apply for a library card and this woman told me I can't have one. I don't understand why. All I want to do is read.'

'What are you interested in?' the young woman continued.

60 'Oh,' Allen began eagerly, 'I'd like to see if there's a biography of Winslow Homer. He's one of my favorite painters. And also I'd like the Thayer two-volume biography of Beethoven.' He was sincere, but he was also trying to impress her. She probably thought he was going to list some novels or murder mysteries.

continued …

65　'Well, Mrs Helms,' the younger woman said, 'since I know those books wouldn't be available at the colored library, I don't think we'd be breaking
70　any rules if we let this young man have a card.'

Allen allowed himself to get happy, but the woman had called him 'young man' and not 'boy', and that made him a little
75　wary. No white woman called a Negro anything but 'boy'.

The old librarian was obviously furious, but she only spluttered, 'Whatever you say, Mrs Macintosh.'

Allen was surprised. The younger librarian was probably in charge of the whole library. The other one probably wasn't even a
80　librarian, but just some ol' white woman who sat there and looked so unpleasant she made people want to read books so they'd forget about her.

'Would you come with me, please?' the younger woman said.

Allen wanted to turn and stick out his tongue at all the white
85　people standing around, but just as he had shown no expression the day he scored twelve points, his face was impassive now. He walked into the woman's office and she handed him a card to fill out.

'These people are funny, aren't they?' she said.

'I beg your pardon?' he replied cautiously.
90　'I mean their silly rules. They think the library will fall if colored people start using it.'

He didn't say anything, knowing that it was particularly unwise to get into conversations with white people when they were talking against other white people. He filled out the card
95　quickly and handed it back to her.

'You're only fourteen?'

'That's right, ' he said pleasantly.

'Aren't you mighty young to be reading such difficult books?'

'I don't think so.'

100 'Well, we'll have to have your mother or father's permission. Take this card home,' she said, handing him another card, 'and have your mother sign it and bring it back as soon as you can. In the meantime I'll make out a temporary card for you so you can take some books out today. When you bring this other card back

105 with your mother's signature, we'll give you a permanent card.' She sat down at the typewriter and quickly typed out the temporary card. 'I don't know if you know it, but you're the first colored person to use this library.'

'I didn't know.'

110 'There shouldn't be any trouble though. But this could cost me my job.'

He felt a little guilty.

'I don't think so,' she continued. 'They had me come down here from Ohio to take this job, and I don't think they'll fire me just yet.'

115 So that was it. She was from the North. He wanted to apologize to her for maybe causing her trouble, but he didn't. He hadn't done anything wrong.

Now answer these questions:

1 Explain where it becomes apparent that there is a problem about Allen using the library.

2 What words, used in the description of the situation down to line 26, 'You people have your own library,' prepare the reader for this open expression of racial prejudice?

3 Explain the mixed nature of Allen's feelings at this point.

4 What does the younger librarian say and do that wins Allen's confidence and reassures him?

5 At the end of the extract why, in your opinion, does Allen feel 'he wanted to apologize'?

Learning about language: *adverbs*

In the same way that an adjective 'modifies' or gives more information about a noun (see Unit 4), **an adverb usually modifies a verb**.

For example: 'She waited' gives the bare facts, but 'She waited patiently' gives a little more information.
'Patiently' is an adverb that says more about how 'she waited'.

■ **Adverbs may also modify adjectives and other adverbs.**

For example: 'David is a sensible boy' includes the adjective 'sensible' to describe the boy, David.
'David is a very sensible boy' makes him seem even more sensible. The adverb 'very' is telling us more about – 'modifying' – the adjective 'sensible'.

Similarly: 'I held the expensive vase carefully' includes the adverb 'carefully' to describe the action of 'holding'.
'I held the expensive vase extremely carefully' emphasises the care being taken. The adverb 'extremely' is telling us more about – modifying – the adverb 'carefully'.

■ **Adverbs describe:**

- **manner** (how) – patiently, quickly, bravely
  She smiled *happily* at everyone in the room.

- **place** (where) – there, everywhere, near
  I've found it *here*, by the sofa.

- **time** (when) – now, soon, then
  They left *today* for a holiday abroad.

- **frequency** (how often) – often, twice, always
  We visit my cousins *occasionally*.

- **degree** (how much) – very, fairly, quite
  My brother does *hardly* any work at all.

- **interrogation** (beginning questions) – why? how? where?
  How do you start the engine?

Skills practice: *recognising adverbs*

Exercise A
Copy out these sentences, highlighting or underlining the adverbs.

1 Our class worked hard for Mr Jain.

2 Drive more slowly, Dad, so I can see what's happening.

3 Stop running immediately!

4 We looked everywhere for the missing book.

5 Where will I find the frying pan?

6 Have you read that book yet?

7 I came top of the class once.

8 Zulfikar copied each word carefully into his book.

9 Tracey was secretly finishing her homework in the back row.

10 I last saw it over there.

Exercise B
Copy out these sentences and complete them with a suitable adverb. Make the sentences as amusing or unusual as you like, provided they still make sense!

1 Becky was writing _____ when the fire alarm went.

2 _____ will the bonfire be lit?

3 Ms Ash was searching _____ for a stick of chalk.

4 Marie denied the allegation _____ .

5 We should be arriving in Bristol _____ .

6 Lyn claimed that she worked _____ .

7 _____ did Adrian open the door?

8 They behaved _____ in a dangerous situation.

9 Everyone treated him _____ after hearing all about the incident from their teacher.

10 United scored _____ in the last minute.

Exercise C
Read the sentences on the next page and then complete the table, indicating what kind of adverb (of manner, place, time, frequency, degree or interrogation) each one is. Look back at the rules to help you. The first one is done for you as an example.

continued …

1 The piece of paper fluttered slowly to the ground.

2 We shall shortly be flying over Istanbul.

3 I thought that boy was quite stupid.

4 Why were you climbing out of the window?

5 Occasionally I wonder if I'm in the right job.

6 The lift went down to the basement.

7 She glanced up to see if anyone was looking.

8 Nanette was watching too.

9 You do that well.

10 Where shall I put these videos?

Sentence/adverb	Kind of adverb
slowly	*manner*
shortly	
quite	
why	
occasionally	
down	
up	
too	
well	
where	

Exercise D

Copy out these sentences, underlining or highlighting an adverb modifying an adjective.

1 That piece of equipment is absolutely useless.

2 How very rough the sea is this morning.

3 The cast was hardly ready when the orchestra started the overture.

4 Mr Henderson gets so angry with those boys.

5 Rajesh was quietly confident as he lined up before the exam.

6 What an amazingly foolish girl you are!

7 I looked across at Gavin, who was almost speechless.

8 Uncle Charles was in a seriously bad way.

9 When I was a lad, I was too lazy for words.

10 Simon is quite intelligent, in fact.

Exercise E

Copy out these sentences, underlining or highlighting an adverb modifying another adverb.

1 We giggled too noisily, which gave the game away.

2 Caroline sat down very suddenly.

3 By half time, we were winning quite easily.

4 Nick has taken off to Scotland once again.

5 They behaved very coolly in such a dangerous situation.

6 How wonderfully well you sing!

7 I've been to Wales twice now.

8 You hardly ever have to remind her to say thank you.

9 Wright played incredibly badly throughout the second half.

10 Tom didn't work quickly enough.

Word building: *adverb suffixes*

■ The most common adverb suffix is '**-ly**' added to the word stem.

For example: the adjective 'slow' forms the adverb 'slow**ly**'.

■ Some word stems form the adverb by adding '**-ily**'.

For example: 'haste' becomes 'hast**ily**'.

■ Some drop the final '-e'.

For example: 'terribl**e**' becomes 'terrib**ly**'.

■ Some words add '**-ally**' to form the adverb.

For example: 'terrific' becomes 'terrific**ally**'.

Refer back to Unit 11 for the spelling rules about the silent '-e'.

(Note: although '-ly' is the most common adverb suffix, remember you have already learned about other adverbs, such as 'everywhere', 'often', 'down' etc. Do not assume that all adverbs end in '-ly', or '-ily' / '-ally', or that all words which have these endings are adverbs.)

Skills practice: *forming adverbs*

Exercise A
Complete this table by forming adverbs from the words given.
The first one is done for you as an example.

Word/stem	Adverb
love	lovely
final	
careful	
real	
complete	
bad	
nice	
perfect	
immediate	
helpful	
legal	

Exercise B
Complete this table by forming adverbs from the words given.
Watch the spelling! The first one is done for you as an example.

Word/stem	Adverb
angry	angrily
remarkable	
extreme	
easy	
complete	
scientific	
hopeful	
busy	
electric	
increasing	
accidental	

Text building: *using brackets and dashes*

Sometimes a writer will include a piece of additional information in a sentence; the information may be interesting but not essential. Such information is said to be 'parenthetical' or 'in parentheses', and various forms of punctuation may be used to show this.

- **The dash is used to separate off an afterthought or an aside at the end of a sentence, when the writer wants to indicate a pause to emphasise a conclusion or create some other effect, such as humour.**

  For example: She played extracts from Rachmaninov, Chopin and Liszt – a brilliant performance.

  'Here thou, great Anna! whom three realms obey, Dost sometimes counsel take – and sometimes tea.'
  (Pope - *The Rape of the Lock*)

- **The dash may also be used to indicate a hesitation in speech.**

  For example: As the officer approached the car, I stammered, 'What – what have I do – done?'

- **Brackets are often used to separate off an additional piece of information within a sentence.**

  For example: Some of the vegetables on display at the village show (carrots, potatoes, marrows) had grown to an enormous size.

  'Pearce as substitute (Wilson having gone off with hamstring trouble) gave new life to the tired forward line.'

The additional piece of information may be an afterthought or an aside, perhaps a passing comment made by the writer to the reader.

For example: Imran's gymnastic routine was so complex, so fast; he is amazingly (I use the word advisedly as my eyes could hardly follow his movements) agile and athletic.

My father (foolish old man that he is!) decided to invest in a motorbike.

- **Pairs of dashes may be used in a similar way to brackets to separate off an additional piece of information within a sentence.** This additional information is still quite closely related to the rest of the sentence, however.

For example: My father – a foolish old man – decided to invest in a motorbike.

Remember: Where the information is very closely related to the rest of the sentence, commas may be used (see Unit 10).

For example: That foolish old man, my father, decided to invest in a motorbike.

- Often the use and choice of brackets, dashes or commas depends on exactly what you wish to say.

- It illustrates the important principle that punctuation is designed to make the writer's meaning absolutely clear to the reader. It provides in precise printed form what might be conveyed in a conversation by tone of voice, gesture and body language.

Skills practice: *using brackets and dashes*

- Copy out these sentences, adding brackets, dashes and commas where you think they are appropriate.
- After each sentence, write a brief explanation of why you have used the punctuation you have added. The first one has been done for you as an example.
- Remember commas are used in lists as well as for other purposes. Example:

    The Grand Hotel has been there for years and its staff are friendly always a novelty in an English hotel.

    (Typical comment: *I would place a dash rather than a comma between 'friendly' and 'always' because the last phrase is separate from the rest of the sentence and is intended to be a bit sarcastic and funny, and a longer pause gives the reader a moment to wait for the punchline.*)

1 The map of the site was dotted with strange names Connaught Mews Chapel Square The Forum that owed little to its previous existence.

2 The 1905-6 team photo which, to this day, hangs in the bar of the clubhouse of the Broomslea Rugby Club features Peter Waite as captain.

3 By then Julie could be excused for tiring after all a girl can only eat so many snacks but on Friday evening she was due to turn up at a yet another wine and cheese evening.

4 Shivering I dug through my rucksack and took out every item of clothing I could find a denim shirt two sweatshirts and an extra pair of jeans.

5 Using the Underground map which people from all parts of the world can understand in a moment they took a Central Line train to Liverpool Street changed to a Circle Line train heading west and travelled straight to their destination.

6 I bet you don't even know whether Simonstown the country's premier naval base is east or west of Cape Town!

Writing

Think back to your discussions about prejudice at the start of this unit and the extract about Allen's experience at the library. Then write an article for your class newspaper/school magazine on this topic:

Describe some of the problems created for young people by the prejudices of others and suggest how these might be dealt with.

 ICT Extra!

Desktop publishing

In the light of the information you have gathered about prejudice, produce a leaflet or poster, setting out rules for avoiding prejudice and/or ways to deal with it. Look back to any DTP work you may have done for Unit 2 and Unit 5. Use the experience you have gained then to assist in producing something colourful, informative and effective.

Unit 14: Join it with conjunctions

In this unit you will:

- read an extract from *Frankenstein*;
- learn about conjunctions;
- learn more about homophones;
- practise proof-reading written work.

Speaking and listening

ICT Extra!

Finding information via the Internet
Use the Internet to find information about hauntings and well-known ghosts –
for example, the ghosts of Borley Rectory or the hauntings at Dover Castle.

- Tell the class a story!

- After a few minutes to think and gather ideas, each member of
  the class in turn tells their classmates about a mysterious or
  spooky experience. It may be something personal or
  something that happened to a friend or relative.

- Recount the experience as clearly and confidently as you can.

Understanding

Writers attempt to build up mood and atmosphere by the words
they choose and the events they create. Read this extract from Mary
Shelley's *Frankenstein* and then answer the question that follows.

*'Frankenstein' is told in the form of a series of letters from Robert
Walton, an English Arctic explorer, to his sister back home in England.
This is the beginning of the fourth letter.*

To Mrs Saville, England

August 5th 17 –

So strange an accident has happened to us that I cannot forbear
recording it, although it is very probable that you will see me
before these papers can come into your possession.

5

Last Monday (July 31st), we were nearly surrounded by ice,
which closed in the ship on all sides, scarcely leaving her the sea-
room in which she floated. Our situation was somewhat
dangerous, especially as we were compassed round by a very
10 thick fog. We accordingly lay to, hoping that some change would
take place in the atmosphere and weather.

About two o'clock the mist cleared away, and we beheld,
stretched out in every direction, vast and irregular plains of ice,
which seemed to have no end. Some of my comrades groaned,
15 and my own mind began to grow watchful with anxious
thoughts, when a strange sight suddenly attracted our attention,
and diverted out solicitude from our own situation. We perceived
a low carriage, fixed on a sledge and drawn by dogs, pass on
towards the north, at the distance of half a mile: a being which
20 had the shape of a man, but apparently of gigantic stature, sat in
the sledge, and guided the dogs. We watched the rapid progress
of the traveller with our telescopes, until he was lost among the
distant inequalities of the ice.

This appearance excited our unqualified wonder. We were, as we
25 believed, many hundred miles from any land; but this apparition
seemed to denote that it was not, in reality,
so distant as we had supposed. Shut in,
however, by ice, it was impossible to
follow his track, which we had observed
30 with the greatest attention.

About two hours after this occurrence,
we heard the ground sea; and before night
the ice broke, and freed our ship. We,
however, lay to until the morning, fearing to encounter in the dark
35 those large, loose masses which float about after the breaking up of
the ice. I profited of this time to rest for a few hours.

In the morning, however, as soon as it was light, I went upon

continued …

deck, and found all the sailors busy on one side of the vessel, apparently talking to some one in the sea. It was, in fact, a sledge,
40 like that we had seen before, which had drifted towards us in the night, on a large fragment of ice. Only one dog remained alive; but there was a human being within it whom the sailors were persuading to enter the vessel. He was not, as the other traveller seemed to be, a savage inhabitant of some undiscovered island,
45 but European. When I appeared on deck, the master said, 'Here is our captain, and he will not allow you to perish on the open sea.'

On perceiving me, the stranger addressed me in English, although with a foreign accent. 'Before I come on board your vessel,' said he, 'will you have the kindness to inform me whither
50 you are bound?'

You may conceive my astonishment on hearing such a question addressed to me from a man on the brink of destruction, and to whom I should have supposed that my vessel would have been a resource which he would not have exchanged for the most
55 precious wealth the Earth can afford. I replied, however, that we were on a voyage of discovery towards the northern pole.

Upon hearing this he appeared satisfied, and consented to come on board. Good God! Margaret, if you had seen the man who thus capitulated for his safety, your surprise
60 would have been boundless. His limbs were nearly frozen, and his body dreadfully emaciated by fatigue and suffering. I never saw a man in so wretched a condition. We attempted to
65 carry him into the cabin; but as soon as he had quitted the fresh air, he fainted. We accordingly brought him back to the deck, and restored him to animation by rubbing him with

70 brandy, and forcing him to swallow a small quantity. As soon as he showed signs of life we wrapped him up in blankets, and placed him near the chimney of the kitchen stove. By slow degrees he recovered, and ate a little soup, which restored him wonderfully.

75   Two days passed in this manner before he was able to speak; and I often feared that his sufferings had deprived him of understanding. When he had in some measure recovered, I removed him to my own cabin, and attended on him as much as my duty would permit. I never saw a more interesting creature:

80 his eyes have generally an expression of wildness, and even madness; but there are moments when, if any one performs an act of kindness towards him, or does him any the most trifling service, his whole countenance is lighted up, as it were, with a beam of benevolence and sweetness that I never saw equalled.

85 But he is generally melancholy and despairing and sometimes he gnashes his teeth, as if impatient of the weight of woes that oppresses him.

Now answer this question:

'So strange an accident has happened to us …' How does Mary Shelley bring out the strangeness of this episode?

You should comment in detail on:

■ the way Walton's surroundings are described;

■ the passing sledge;

■ the circumstances in which the stranger comes aboard;

■ the description of the stranger and his first two days on board.

Remember to refer to particular details, words and phrases from the passage to support your comments.

Learning about language: *conjunctions*

Conjunctions are 'joining words', used to bring together words, phrases or clauses.

1 Co-ordinating conjunctions connect one item or idea with another, giving both items equal status – i.e. one is not more important than or dependent upon the other. The most common co-ordinating conjunctions are 'and', 'but' and 'or'.

For example: 'I sat down at my desk and she sat down at hers' is a sentence with two simple items or ideas: 'I sat down at my desk' and 'She sat down at her desk'. Both items have equal status; her sitting down does not depend upon my sitting down, or vice versa.

■ **'And'** is used to bring together two or more similar items or ideas; **'but'** is used to bring together two different items or ideas, neither of which depends on the other.

For example: 'I sat down at my desk but she remained standing by the door' emphasises the difference between one person sitting down and one remaining standing, but one action does not depend on, or result from, the other.

■ **'Or'** is used to bring together two or more alternative items or ideas, again, where one does not depend on the other.

For example: 'Will you go to Edinburgh or Glasgow?' gives two alternatives; going to Edinburgh does not depend on going – or not going, for that matter – to Glasgow, and it may be that you will go to both.

■ Other common co-ordinating conjunctions are: **'either … or'**; **'neither … nor'**; and **'both … and'** – all of which operate as a pair.

For example: Either Sean Connery or Roger Moore was playing James Bond.
Gill could eat neither cheese nor chocolate.
He has both the time and the money to play polo.

2 **Subordinating conjunctions connect items or ideas which are not given equal status because one is dependent upon or reveals more about the main item or idea.** Therefore, the clauses such conjunctions introduce are called subordinate clauses because they give more information about the main clause.

The most common are subordinating conjunctions of:

■ **reason: because, for, as, since** – i.e. introducing a reason or explanation of why something happens

For example: I came to school on the bus because it was raining.
She took the food eagerly, for she had eaten nothing since the morning.
We had to walk all the way as we had no money for bus fares.
Since it was so warm, we took off our sweatshirts.

■ **time: before, after, until, when, while, as, since** – i.e. introducing some idea of when something happens

For example: Lyn watched *Neighbours* before doing her homework.
After washing up, Dad sat in the armchair and dozed.
No one will leave the room until the culprit has owned up.
When we lived in the country, we weren't able to go to the cinema very often.
Sophie was humming quietly to herself while she finished the ironing.
As darkness fell, it grew much colder.
Since that holiday in Italy, I have never liked spaghetti.

(Note: 'as' and 'since' have more than one meaning and use. They can also be used to mean 'because'.)

■ **place: where, wherever** – i.e. introducing some idea of where something happens

For example: My father never knows where he is going.
Wherever I turn, I find the baby's toys spread over the floor.

■ **condition: if** – i.e. introducing some idea of what conditions allow something to happen

For example: If you pay attention, you may learn something to your advantage.

■ **concession: though, although, however, in spite of** – i.e. introducing some idea of a contrast between what might be expected to happen and what does happen, or even surprise that something happens

For example: To be fair, he did listen to me patiently, though he was very angry.
Although that piece of work is in pencil, I suppose I'll mark it.
However upset she may have been, she still showed no sign of emotion.
He managed to eat an enormous meal in spite of his illness.

■ **purpose: to, in order to** – i.e. introducing some idea of an intention to make something happen

For example: We travelled up to London to do our Christmas shopping.
Matthew walked home through the back streets in order to avoid being seen by his friends.

■ **result: so that** – i.e. introducing some idea of an achieved intention

For example: Robyn had set off early so that she would not miss the train.

Skills practice: *using conjunctions*

Exercise A
Join these sentences with a co-ordinating conjunction. Check back to the examples on page 148. You may need to leave some words out or make changes to the word order.

1 Dad was annoyed. Mum thought it was funny.
2 Ryan can play in midfield. Ryan can play up-front.
3 Kevin likes French. He also likes German.
4 Christmas Day is 25th December. My birthday is 25th December.
5 I had fish and chips. Sharon had pie and peas.
6 Hemant is qualified to play for India. He is qualified to play for England.
7 Charles cannot understand Pythagoras. Andrew isn't sure about Pythagoras.
8 In the test, Alex could not spell 'beautiful'. Alastair could not spell 'beautiful'.
9 Tracey was going out with Dean. Jamie was going out Jenny.
10 I last saw it over there. Jason last saw it over here.

Exercise B
Join these sentences with a subordinating conjunction of time. Check the examples on page 149. You may need to leave some words out or make changes to the word order and verb forms.

1 Becky was writing a letter. Suddenly the fire alarm sounded.
2 John was concentrating on his jigsaw puzzle. Finally the last piece was put in its place.
3 Zoe washed her hair. Later she put on her make-up.
4 Jackie finally succeeded in turning the key. She had been trying a long time.
5 Gary left the house. He remembered to lock the door.
6 Lynn was playing with some building bricks. At the same time, Alice was banging her drum.
7 I had mumps when I was young. I am a little deaf.
8 Stay where you are. I will tell you when to leave.
9 I switched off the light. I left the room.
10 Many of the fans drifted away. Arsenal scored the winning goal

Exercise C
Complete these sentences with a subordinating conjunction of reason or place. Look back at the examples on page 149. You may need to leave some words out or make changes to the word order and verb forms.

1 _____ Mary went, her dog followed.

2 You tell me the answer, Greg, _____ you have whispered it to half the class already.

3 Mr Ahmed has been appointed _____ he performed well at interview.

4 The days were short, _____ it was now December.

5 _____ he claimed to be his long lost brother, Nick let him stay.

6 Can you remember _____ we went on holiday to Corfu?

7 I am sending your daughter home _____ she hit another girl.

8 _____ it's your bat, you can bat first.

9 The river is dangerous at this point _____ the currents are strong.

Exercise D
Complete these sentences with a subordinating conjunction of condition, concession, purpose or result. Look at the examples on page 150.

1 _____ she is only 14 years old, she has won a place at Oxford.

2 We finally managed to win _____ of being two men short.

3 I went to the supermarket _____ to stock up with everything for the holiday.

4 _____ you keep having dreams like that, you should stop eating cheese at bedtime.

5 Tony had a Saturday job _____ save up for a new computer.

6 Laurie sang loudly _____ everyone knew he was having a bath.

7 _____ exhausted you might be, you can still make me a cup of tea.

8 _____ he speaks no English, he always makes himself understood.

9 We enjoyed ourselves _____ the weather.

10 Katie jumped up on a chair _____ everyone could see her.

Word building: *spelling rules: homophones*

In Unit 12, you learned about some words, called homophones, that are easy to confuse because of their similar sounds. Here are some more homophones; check that you know the difference between the words in each pair. One set has three similar sounding words!

aloud	allowed	groan	grown
bare	bear	hair	hare
brake	break	heal	heel
by	buy		

here	hear	piece	peace
mail	male	pray	prey
meet	meat	right	write
moan	mown		

rain	rein	reign
see	sea	
some	sum	
wait	weight	
week	weak	
weather	whether	

Skills practice: *homophones*

Exercise A
Complete these sentences with the correct word chosen from the first block of words shown above (aloud/allowed to heal/heel).

1 I heard a strange cry, like a _____ , from behind the hedge.

2 Her _____ arms had caught the sun really badly.

3 I'm going into town to _____ my Christmas presents.

4 Are you able to meet me at _____ this morning?

5 There's a hole in the _____ of my sock.

continued ...

6 Younger pupils are not _____ to leave the school premises at lunchtime.

7 He has the most amazingly long, blond _____ .

8 The back _____ block on my bike is broken.

9 My younger sister has _____ three inches in the last six months.

10 How long will it take for the wound to _____ ?

Exercise B

Complete these sentences with the correct word chosen from the second block of words on page 153 (here/hear to right/write).

1 Has the postman delivered any _____ this morning?

2 Please _____ the answers to these questions for homework.

3 Will you have a _____ of this delicious _____ pie?

4 I'll _____ you by the school gates at three o'clock.

5 Did you _____ what I said?

6 Let us _____ for people less fortunate than ourselves.

7 Take the first left and then the third _____ and you'll see the shop straight in front of you.

8 Have you _____ the lawn this week?

9 The Welsh have the best _____ voice choirs.

10 It's nine o'clock and _____ is the news.

Exercise C

Complete these sentences with the correct word chosen from the third block of words on page 153 (rain/rein/reign to weather/whether).

1 I asked _____ there would be any chance of an extra ticket.

2 He was so _____ after the operation, he had to stay in hospital for over a _____ .

3 Please find me _____ more samples than that.

4 I may be kept in detention, so don't _____ for me.

5 The _____ of King George VI ended in 1952.

6 The _____ has been very dry this summer, but _____ is forecast for the autumn.

7 Please _____ in your enthusiasm for football until the end of the lesson.

8 I can tell you've been eating too much over Christmas because I can _____ you've put on _____ again.

9 I used to find _____ difficult even when I was at my other school.

10 All that bad _____ yesterday made the _____ really rough.

Text building: *standard English and proof-reading*

By 'standard English' we mean that form of English which is written and spoken according to agreed rules and conventions of grammar, spelling and punctuation.

While people may speak with different accents and use words and phrases from local dialects, these are used in written work only to achieve particular effects, for example, in building characters.

In your written work, therefore, you will be mainly concerned with writing accurate standard English. Most of the text building activities so far have focused on issues such as grammatical accuracy and the use of punctuation to make meaning clear.

Your understanding of the rules and conventions of standard English, and of what is required to communicate meaning precisely, must be applied to your own writing to improve its quality and effectiveness. Therefore, you must get into the habit of checking – **proof-reading** – your work to make sure there are no errors and the meaning is clear. This is the last stage of the drafting and re-drafting of your work, to ensure that the final version is as good as you can make it.

Proof-reading checklist:

- **Sentence markers.** Are there commas where there should be full stops? Are there full stops where there should be question marks?

- **Speech.** Have you used all the usual conventions correctly? (Check back to Unit 7.)

- **Other punctuation.** Are commas, semi-colons, dashes, etc. where they should be?

- **Spelling.** Have you observed the 'i' before 'e' rule? (Check back to Unit 8.) Have you formed word endings correctly? Have you confused any homophones, e.g. written 'no' for 'know'?

- **Verbs.** Have you used the right tenses? If you have changed tense or used conditionals, have you used the right forms of the verb?

■ **Auxiliary and modal verbs.** Have you used the right forms so that you say exactly what you mean?

Skills practice: *standard English and proof-reading*

Below is a piece of writing by a Year 9 pupil who handed it in to the teacher without carrying out any of these checks.

■ Rewrite it, correcting the mistakes.

■ If you think you can improve the way things have been expressed, you may make those sorts of changes as well.

■ When you have finished, write a report explaining all the changes you have made and why.

 ICT Extra!

Computer spelling and grammar checkers.
How much use can you make of these facilities? Do you have to enter whole chunks of text to take advantage of this sort of help? How useful are these checkers?

Black Magic in Barnsley

She approached the old church warily. She was not a religious woman, but ruined buildings worried her She became even more worried when she heard the strange chanting coming from inside. she slipped cautiously threw the doorway into the black heart of the church. There was a group of people hunched around the old altar, one of them was holding something aloft in both hands. Light glinted of the edge off it.

What is it, Maureen wondered to herself as she continued towards the figures. There was an unearthly squeal.

'STOP!' she yelled.

The figures turned around at once. The one holding the knife for that was what it was droped it. To Maureens complete surprise they were all old women pensioners.

She even reconised the woman with the unpriced pilchards, who was sporting a false boil. At that moment Mrs beasley's cat Lucky jumped off the alter and landed just in front of her. Considering it had nearly been stabed to death, its name seemed appropriate.

Maureen was stunned.

WHO THE HELL ARE YOU?' she demanded.

The old women shuffled nervously and looked at one another. After a couple of minutes one of them came forward.

'We're the Athersley Pensioners' Beetledrive and Occult Witchcraft Group.' she proudly announced. 'My name's Mrs Halliwell - I'm the leader of our coven.' She indicated a thin, shriveled up woman with pince-nez and overdone black eyeliner. 'This is Mrs Jones,' she told Maureen. They shook hands limply. 'And Mrs McKinley,' she pointed to a fat, jolly looking woman. 'And lastly, Mrs Easterbury,' who Maureen recognised as the pilchard lady. 'I'm afraid there's only four of us – we're a bit short handed for a coven.'

Writing

- Think back to the mysterious and spooky stories told by your class at the beginning of this unit. Then look back at the *Frankenstein* mystery and *Black Magic in Barnsley*.

- Now write two or three opening paragraphs, setting the scene for your own mystery story. Concentrate on creating mood and atmosphere.

Unit 15: Poetry and paragraphs

In this unit you will:

- read a poem;
- learn about pronouns;
- learn about word origins;
- learn about and practise organising written work in paragraphs.

Speaking and listening

- This activity needs some preparation. You will need to work in groups of four, each divided into two pairs.

- Each pair should find a large newspaper article, cut it out from the paper and then cut the article up into separate paragraphs.

- Make sure you label each paragraph so you can put the article together again when you need to, but number the paragraphs in a random order which you keep a note of.

- Swap your collection of paragraphs with the other pair. Each pair must try to sort them into the right order by reading them and making sense of the whole article.

- When each pair has put their article together, check with your opposite pair to see if you have done it correctly.

- What clues did you find in the article – e.g. particular words, the way the subject matter was organised – to help you sort it out?

Understanding

A constant theme in this book has been that writers choose words carefully. This is nowhere more true than in the writing of poetry, which brings together not just choice of words, but many other complex elements like rhythm, rhyme and verse pattern as well as verb forms, punctuation, sentence structure, etc.

There is not sufficient scope here to examine the various forms of poetry as fully as might be wished, but the essential quality of all poetry is its 'compactness'. A novel, a play, even a short story, is usually much longer than a poem. The poet is trying to capture a mood, create an effect or explore a thought or idea in very few words, comparatively speaking.

Consequently, the words in a poem are more likely to be tightly packed with meaning, with their sounds, their structure and the associations they carry with them all contributing to the effect the poet wishes to create. For the same reasons, poets tend to rely heavily on ambiguity, imagery (see Unit 19) and symbolism to define and clarify their ideas. Hence, a poem usually requires more detailed examination and closer study than prose if you are really to understand it.

The best approach to a poem may, therefore, be to read it through quite quickly a couple of times to gather the general drift of what the poet is saying. Then look more closely and try to work out the separate ideas or aspects of the poet's thoughts as they build up, possibly listing these in note form. Finally, as your overall picture of what the poet is saying becomes more certain, the significance of particular words and phrases will become clearer to you and you can begin to appreciate in detail exactly what the poem means.

Read this poem by Enid Barraclough, called *Procrastination*. It is a comparatively straightforward poem in a free verse style about the difficulties of keeping up a friendship.

'It is difficult to pick up
A thing you have let go –
A ball – bouncing out of sight –
The string of a kite
5 That sails away in the wind,
But most of all a friend
Neglected, lost to view
And almost out of mind.
The writing pad is near at hand
10 The pen invites you but
You hesitate, it is so long –
How can you break the barrier
Of time you both have built?
Your hand is on the telephone,
15 It rings, and someone else's voice
Deters you from the link you
Would have forged. Days go by,

continued ...

The thought still in your mind
At intervals, but you do not
20 Make the move. Sometimes you think
Why should I be the first
To bridge the gap? You thrust away
The instinct of a friend –
Or else you fear that
25 You may meet rebuff.
And so the overture
Is never made. How sad
That friendships die
For lack of nurture. So much
30 Love is wasted in the air.
It is difficult to pick up
A thing you have let go,
Hard to retrieve
So delicate a thing
35 Held by so tenuous a thread,
That gone beyond recall
It breaks –
You only had to lift the telephone.

Now answer these questions:

1 What happens to a ball, a kite and a neglected friend? (lines 3–8)

2 How does what happens help to make clear the poet's statement in the first two lines?

3 With the writing pad near and the pen inviting (lines 9–10), what prevents the writing of a letter?

4 What is suggested by the word 'barrier'? (line 12)

5 What hinders the making of a telephone call? (lines 14–17)

6 What other reasons are given (lines 17–25) for the fact that 'the overture is never made'?

7 What is the effect of the word 'nurture'? (line 29)

8 How does the ending of the poem (lines 31–38) develop the thoughts expressed at the beginning?

9 Why, in the opinion of the writer, do 'friendships die'?

10 Explain what you think the writer's feelings about friendship are in this poem.

Learning about language: *pronouns*

A pronoun is a word that may be used to replace a noun, in order to avoid repeating the noun.

For example: Maria was in class. She was sitting at the back.

In the second of these two sentences, 'she' is a **personal pronoun** that saves the writer from having to repeat 'Maria'.

Pronouns make your writing more fluent and effective by avoiding unnecessary repetition. However, you must make it clear to what/to whom the pronoun refers.

For example: Peter and Alan were chasing Chris. Then he smacked him.

Here, the use of pronouns leaves the reader confused about who 'smacked' whom, so instead of making the writing more fluent, it confuses it.

1 **Personal pronouns:**

(a) **I, you, he, she, it, we, they – may be used in place of a noun that is the subject of a sentence.**

(b) **me, you, him, her, it, us, them – may be used in place of a noun that is the object of a sentence.**

(Check back to Unit 1 if you are not sure about the difference between a subject and an object.)

For example: **We** (subject) were throwing the ball to each other.
Tom likes **them** (object).

2 **Reflexive pronouns – myself, yourself, yourselves, himself, herself, itself, ourselves, themselves –** are used for emphasis and refer back to ('reflect') the subject of the sentence.

For example: In the end, I did it myself.
Those girls can only blame themselves for being in detention.

3   **Possessive pronouns – mine, yours, his, hers, ours, theirs –** are used to show who owns or possesses something.

For example: This pen is mine. Have you got yours?

(Note: some people classify words like my, your, his, her, their [which in foreign languages may be called 'possessive adjectives'] as possessive pronouns. These words are more often referred to as 'possessive determiners' in modern grammar.)

4   **Demonstrative pronouns – this, that, these, those –** are used to draw attention to something, usually indicating its closeness to the speaker.

For example: This is the happiest day of my life.

That was a miserable day.

5   **Indefinite pronouns – no one, nobody, nothing, someone, somebody, something, anyone, anybody, anything, everyone, everybody, everything –** are used to refer to a person or object without saying precisely who or what.

For example: Everybody enjoyed themselves at Linda's party.

There's nothing I can do to help.

6   **Interrogative pronouns – who, whom, whose, what, which –** are used to express questions.

Who is used when asking about the person who is the subject of the sentence.

For example: Who took my pencil?

Whom is used when the person is the object of the sentence, and after prepositions. (Check Unit 16 for more about prepositions.)

For example: Whom did you see?
                With whom did you go to the concert?

(Note: 'whom' is frequently replaced by 'who' when the preposition is moved to the end of the sentence. For example: 'Who did you go to the concert with?')

Whose is used to discover ownership or possession.

For example: Whose are these sandwiches?

What is used for things.

For example: What did you see?

Which may be used for people or objects when there are only a few to choose from.

For example: Which do you want?

(Note: 'whose', 'what' and 'which' are also possessive adjectives/determiners. For example: 'Whose sandwiches are these?'; 'What boys did you see?'; 'Which shirt do you want?')

7 **Relative pronouns – who, whom, whose, which, that –** refer to a noun and introduce a clause that gives more information about that noun. These clauses are called relative clauses; they are another type of subordinate clause.

For example: The man who (**subject**) robbed you is called Edwards.

The man whom (**object**) you saw is called Jackson.

The man from whom I bought it is called Evans.

The man whose dog bit my leg is called Hunter.

The ladder on which I was standing began to slide **or**

The ladder which I was standing on began to slide.

The car that I hired broke down.

(Note: 'which' and 'that' are often interchangeable for objects and may even be left out altogether, especially in conversation. For example: The ladder (that) I was standing on began to slide.)

Skills practice: *using pronouns*

Exercise A

Copy out these sentences, replacing the words in brackets with the correct personal pronoun. Check back to the examples if you need help.

1 Dad was angry because of what (the boys) had said.

2 (Katie) stormed out of the room in a temper.

3 Chris threw (the book) on the table.

4 (My sister and I) are going to India for six weeks.

continued ...

5 I lent (those jeans) to my sister.

6 The storm broke over (Mum and me) as we crossed the field.

7 (Charles) cannot understand why his parents are so pleased.

8 (Paper 2) was the most difficult part of the test.

9 The head teacher sent for (John) after lunch.

10 I walked up to (Mark) and asked for my pen back.

Exercise B

Copy out these sentences, completing them with a reflexive pronoun.
Check the examples for help.

1 You rather shot _____ in the foot with that comment.

2 John was intent on doing the whole thing _____ without anyone else's help.

3 I decided to tackle the washing up _____ .

4 Jackie and Kirsten went off to the party by _____ .

5 You should all consider _____ very lucky that you are not in detention.

6 You will have to leave the cat to take care of _____ for the day.

7 I _____ had measles when I was younger.

8 Shabir and I blamed _____ for giving away that goal.

9 They paid for the whole thing _____ .

10 Mandy has a very high opinion of _____ .

Exercise C

Copy out and complete these sentences with a possessive
pronoun. Check back to the examples if you need help.

1 Rachel introduced me to a brother of _____ .

2 'The classroom along here is _____ ,' said the twins.

3 I was sure that present would be _____ .

4 'It wasn't my fault,' said Darren, 'it was _____ .'

5 I was playing on my computer and Gareth was playing on _____ .

6 May I introduce you to a friend of _____ ?

7 I've already had my holiday, but my parents are taking _____ in October.

8 Tom found his books but Sharon never found _____ .

9 'That box of sweets is _____ ,' I insisted.

10 You eat _____ and then I'll eat _____ .

Exercise D

Copy out these sentences, replacing the words in brackets with a demonstrative pronoun. Look at the examples again if you need help.

1 I bought (the expensive boots) although I did like the other pair.
2 (The trainers on the market stall) are the cheapest trainers in town.
3 (The new party dress) was such a bargain.
4 (The books over there on the shelf) are Lisa's.
5 What is (your homework) doing in the waste-bin?
6 (The pupils) who are responsible will be in trouble.
7 I threw (my old jeans) away last week.
8 Could you see if (my new mouse) works?
9 My mother had saved (the stale buns) for the birds.
10 '(Copying someone else's homework) is wrong,' said Caroline.

Exercise E

Copy out these sentences and complete them with an indefinite pronoun. Look at the examples again, if you need help.

1 _____ there?
2 Can I get you _____ from the shops?
3 You can see they took _____ from this room.
4 _____ applauded wildly at the end of the concert.
5 Mum said, '_____ has been eating my chocolates.'
6 Please make sure that _____ is touched until the police arrive.
7 Has _____ been arrested yet?
8 The school was finally silent because _____ had gone home.
9 _____ will leave the room until the guilty party owns up.
10 _____ must know who is responsible.

Exercise F

Copy out these sentences and complete them with an interrogative pronoun. Check back to the examples if you need to.

1 _____ has been sitting on my chair?
2 _____ is this grubby piece of work?
3 _____ is the longest river in England?
4 To _____ do we owe this lovely meal?
5 _____ do you want to do next?
6 _____ of these proposals will you support?
7 On _____ were you relying for information?

continued ...

8 _____ did you help?

9 _____ university did she go to, Oxford or Cambridge?

10 _____ is the capital city of Poland?

Exercise G

Use a relative pronoun to join the two short sentences into one longer one. If you need to, you may rearrange the word order, leave out some words and change the verb forms. Check back to the examples if you need help.

1 A man reported the accident. He had red hair.

2 A girl in Year 9 told me. She refused to give her name.

3 The head teacher interviewed Andrew. His bullying had been the cause of all the trouble.

4 The old oak tree blew down last night. I had intended to cut it down.

5 *Julius Caesar* was written by Shakespeare. We are going to see the play tomorrow.

6 This can of drink cost 95 pence. It tastes off.

7 Chopin composed some of his music here. His works are world famous.

8 I came home with Liz and her father. He drives a Jaguar.

9 The milk had gone off. It had stood out in the sun too long.

10 We invited our neighbour round for supper. She is a lonely elderly woman.

Word building: *-ology words*

Most of the suffixes you have learned about so far have changed the grammatical form of the word stem – noun/verb to adjective, adverb, etc.

However, new words are often formed by taking parts of words from other languages – usually Latin and Greek – and bringing them together.

■ The suffix **'–logue'** comes from the Greek 'logos', meaning speech. When combined with other words of similar origin, it forms a family of words to do with speaking.

For example: **'mono'** is a Greek stem meaning 'one' or 'alone'
'mono' + 'logue' forms 'monologue' – a long speech or recitation by one person

■ The suffix **'-ology'** means 'the study of' or 'the science of'. When combined with other Latin or Greek word stems, it forms a whole family of words which are the names of branches of science.

For example: **'bios'** is a Greek stem meaning 'life'

'bios' + 'ology' forms 'biology' – the study of living things

Skills practice: *word formation*

Using the following information about Latin and Greek word-stems, complete the table of definitions. You may find it helpful to refer to a dictionary. The list of –ology words is given after the table, so check your answers afterwards.

anthropos	=	man		archaios	=	old
aster	=	star		chronos	=	time
cosmos	=	world/universe		crimen	=	offence/crime
etymos	=	true/origin		geo	=	earth
gyne	=	woman		immunis	=	exempt
ont	=	being		ornis	=	bird
palaeo	=	ancient		pathos	=	suffering/disease
psyche	=	spirit/mind		spelaion	=	cave
techne	=	art		theos	=	god/divinity
zoon	=	animal				

Definitions	–ology words
The study of the stars of the zodiac	astrology
The study of man and society	
The study of diseases	
The study of living things	
The study of women's diseases	
The study of animals	
The study of historical ruins	
The study of the Earth's crust	
The study of the mind	
The study of immunity from disease	
The study of the origin and history of words	

continued ...

The study and exploration of caves
The study of religious beliefs
The study of crime and criminals
The study of birds
The study of mechanical arts
The study of the universe
The study of ancient life through rock strata
The study of events in time order

anthropology	archaeology	astrology	biology
chronology	cosmology	criminology	etymology
geology	gynaecology	immunology	ornithology
palaeontology	pathology	psychology	speleology
technology	theology	zoology	

Text building: *paragraphing, sequencing and structuring*

■ **A paragraph is a group of sentences, or sometimes a single sentence, that forms a unit. The sentences in a paragraph are usually related in some way because they all revolve around one main idea.**

Almost any piece of writing is divided into paragraphs.

Paragraphing helps the reader. When one paragraph ends and a new paragraph begins, the reader knows another aspect of the subject is being dealt with. A new idea needs a new paragraph. This helps the reader follow the story, the argument or whatever the subject matter may be.

Paragraphing also helps give your writing structure or organisation. If a piece of writing is well constructed, it should be possible to summarise the point of each paragraph in a few words or phrases. Everything in that paragraph should be relevant to that point.

A good way to make the meaning of each paragraph clear is to **state the main idea clearly in a 'topic sentence'.** All the other sentences in that paragraph may be related to that statement or topic sentence.

- **'Sequencing' means grouping or organising your paragraphs to make your subject matter easily understood and persuasive to the reader.**

The commonest – and often the best – way to **present material is in chronological order**. This is the method normally used in stories, cookbooks and instructions, for example. Sometimes, however, writers use 'flashback' and other similar devices to produce sequences of events that are not simply chronological.

In non-narrative writing (writing which is not telling a story, e.g. reports, discussions) it is particularly important to **organise your material logically**, so the reader may follow your line of thought. You may:

- identify distinctive characteristics of a topic;
- group similar items;
- analyse similarities and differences;
- give relevant examples;
- comment on actions and reactions;
- suggest solutions to problems.

It is unlikely that one piece of writing will include all these elements, but be sure you link them in a way that makes your meaning clear and easy to follow.

- **Structuring involves 'internal coherence' within paragraphs (making each paragraph's structure clear by linking sentences) and 'overall coherence' (making the whole piece of writing clear by linking paragraphs).**

Internal coherence within paragraphs may be achieved by:

- *repeating key words or phrases* – this not only links sentences but alerts the reader to key points.

For example: a paragraph about teachers' salaries might include words like **'pay'**, **'cost of living'**, **'spending'**, **'hard-earned money'**.

■ *using similar grammatical forms to emphasise the connection between related items*

For example: **'If I ..., then ...; on the other hand, if I ..., then ...'**

■ *using subordinate clauses to link sentences with connected ideas*

For example: **'Although** he ...'; 'She achieved so much **because ...'**;

■ *using pronouns* – because they refer back to nouns, they lead the reader from one sentence to another.

For example: Peter is really keen on Suzie, so **he** is always pleased to carry **her** schoolbag.

Overall coherence between paragraphs may be signalled by:

■ *continuation* – 'also', 'moreover', 'firstly', 'secondly', etc.

■ *passage of time* – 'later', 'after a few days', 'immediately', etc.

■ *comparison* – 'likewise', 'in the same way', 'similarly', etc.

■ *contrast* – 'however', 'in contrast', 'on the other hand', etc.

■ *using examples* – 'for example', 'for instance', 'such as', etc.

■ *showing results* – 'as a result', 'hence', 'accordingly', etc.

■ *position* – 'farther off', 'opposite', 'nearby', etc.

■ *summary/repetition/conclusion* – 'all in all', 'as we have seen', 'in conclusion', etc.

Skills practice: *paragraphing, sequencing and structuring*

Exercise A

Choose one of your recent pieces of writing and look back through it.

1 Have you written in paragraphs? If not, try to identify where your subject moves on and where you should have started a new paragraph.

2 Identify and list the topic sentences in each paragraph you have/should have written. Are they easy to find or are you having to summarise the main points now?

3 Decide which is the weakest paragraph in this respect and list what you could do to make its point more effectively.

Exercise B

Look at your weakest paragraph.

1 List any devices you have used to link ideas and sentences. Can you find any?

2 Decide which ideas and sentences could have been better linked and rewrite them.

Exercise C

Look at your list of topic sentences.

1 When written as a list does their order make sense? Do you get a clear idea of the overall point of the piece of writing?

2 What linking devices have you used to join paragraphs and guide the reader through the subject matter?

3 Identify three places where you could have signalled the next stage of your subject more effectively. Rewrite the first sentence of each of those paragraphs.

Writing

■ With a partner, brainstorm ideas for an amusing piece of writing on the subject 'Friends I have known and hated!'

■ When you have jotted down all your ideas, group those that go together.

■ Write a topic sentence for each group and put them into a sequence. Write each topic sentence on a separate slip of paper and swap sets with another pair.

■ Work out a sequence for the other pair's topic sentences. When you have finished, compare notes and see how far you agree.

■ Decide jointly on a final 'best sequence', and save it for writing up later.

Unit 16: Find an opening

In this unit you will:

- read an extract from Shakespeare's *Macbeth*;
- learn about prepositions;
- learn about prefixes;
- learn about and practise openings for your written work.

Speaking and listening

- Working with a partner, read the scene from *Macbeth* in the next section.

- Once you have the general idea of what is happening and being said, go through the scene in detail, helping each other to work out the precise meaning of what is said and to sort out any difficulties with the Shakespearean language.

Understanding

It is easy to forget that Shakespeare wrote his plays to be performed. His highly charged poetry creates many tense and dramatic confrontations between characters whose real feelings and motives are hinted at rather than explicitly stated.

Read *Macbeth* Act 1, Scene 5 and answer the questions that follow:

In this scene, Lady Macbeth receives a letter from her husband, who is on his way home from battle, telling her about a mysterious meeting with three witches. They have prophesied that he will become Thane (Earl) of Cawdor and later King of Scotland. Almost immediately, King Duncan confers the title of Thane of Cawdor on Macbeth and now Lady Macbeth starts to wonder how the second prophecy might be fulfilled.

Inverness. A room in MACBETH'S *castle.*

Enter LADY MACBETH *alone, with a letter.*

LADY MACBETH

'They met me in the day of success; and I have learn'd by the
5 perfect'st report, they have more in them than mortal knowledge.

When I burnt in desire to
question them further, they made
themselves air, into which they
vanish'd. Whiles I stood rapt in
10 the wonder of it, came missives
from the King, who all-hail'd me
"Thane of Cawdor;" by which
title, before, these weird sisters
saluted me, and referr'd me to the

15 coming on of time, with "Hail, King that shalt be!" This have I
thought good to deliver thee, my dearest partner of greatness, that
thou mightst not lose the dues of rejoicing, by being ignorant of
what greatness is promised thee. Lay it to thy heart, and farewell.'
Glamis thou art, and Cawdor; and shalt be what thou art
20 promised. Yet do I fear thy nature;
It is too full o' th' milk of human kindness
To catch the nearest way. Thou wouldst be great;
Art not without ambition; but without
The illness should attend it. What thou wouldst highly,
25 That wouldst thou holily; wouldst not play false,
And yet wouldst wrongly win. Thou'ldst have, great Glamis,
That which cries 'Thus thou must do, if thou have it;
And that which rather thou dost fear to do
Than wishest should be undone.' Hie thee hither,
30 That I may pour my spirits in thine ear;
And chastise with the valour of my tongue
All that impedes thee from the golden round,
Which fate and metaphysical aid doth seem
To have thee crown'd withal.
35 *Enter a* MESSENGER.
LADY MACBETH
What is your tidings?

continued …

MESSENGER

The King comes here to-night.

40 LADY MACBETH

Thou'rt mad to say it.

Is not thy master with him? who, were't so,

Would have inform'd for preparation.

MESSENGER

45 So please you, it is true. Our Thane is coming.

One of my fellows had the speed of him;

Who, almost dead for breath, had scarcely more

Than would make up his message.

LADY MACBETH

50 Give him tending;

He brings great news.

Exit MESSENGER

The raven himself is hoarse

That croaks the fatal entrance of Duncan

55 Under my battlements. Come, you spirits

That tend on mortal thoughts, unsex me here;

And fill me, from the crown to the toe, top-full

Of direst cruelty! Make thick my blood,

Stop up th'access and passage to remorse,

60 That no compunctious visitings of nature

Shake my fell purpose, nor keep peace between

Th' effect and it! Come to my woman's breasts,

And take my milk for gall, you murd'ring ministers,

Wherever in your sightless substances

65 You wait on nature's mischief! Come, thick night,

And pall thee in the dunnest smoke of hell,

That my keen knife see not the wound it makes,

Nor heaven peep through the blanket of the dark,

To cry 'Hold, hold!'

70 *Enter* MACBETH

LADY MACBETH

Great Glamis! Worthy Cawdor!

Greater than both, by the all-hail hereafter!

Thy letters have transported me beyond

75 This ignorant present, and I feel now

The future in the instant.

MACBETH

My dearest love, Duncan comes here to-night.

LADY MACBETH

80 And when goes hence?

MACBETH

To-morrow, as he purposes.

LADY MACBETH

O, never

85 Shall sun that morrow see!

Your face, my thane, is as a book where men

May read strange matters. To beguile the time,

Look like the time; bear welcome in your eye,

Your hand, your tongue; look like the innocent flower,

90 But be the serpent under't. He that's coming

Must be provided for; and you shall put

This night's great business into my dispatch;

Which shall to all our nights and days to come

Give solely sovereign sway and masterdom.

95 MACBETH

We will speak further.

LADY MACBETH

Only look up clear;

To alter favour ever is to fear.

100 Leave all the rest to me.

Exeunt.

Now answer this question:

What advice would you give the people playing the characters of Lady Macbeth and Macbeth on how to perform their parts in this scene?

You should think about:

● what you learn of the characters of Lady Macbeth and Macbeth from Lady Macbeth's first speech (lines 19–34);

● the significance of Lady Macbeth's reaction to the news that King Duncan is going to spend the night at their castle (lines 53–69);

● what effect is created by such statements as:

'I feel now the future in the instant.'
'O never shall sun that morrow see!'
'Look like the innocent flower but be the serpent under't.'
'He that's coming must be provided for.'
'Leave all the rest to me.'

(Note: you might find it helpful to glance back to the introduction to the extract from Our Day Out *in Unit 11.)*

Learning about language: *prepositions*

■ **A preposition is used to show the relationship – usually in time or place – between nouns or pronouns and other parts of a sentence.**

For example: We did not want to leave **during** the game.

Drive **across** the bridge, go **down** the lane and turn left **past** the filling station.

Good writers check their work **with** great care.

The most common prepositions are:

about	above	across	after	against
along	among	around	as	at
below	before	behind	beneath	beside
between	beyond	by	down	during
except	for	from	in	inside

into	like	near	of	off
on	onto	out	over	past
regarding	since	through	toward	under
until	up	with	without	

■ Sometimes pairs of prepositions are confused in use, so watch out for:

– **for, since**

I have been learning French for three years. (i.e. for a period of time)

I have been learning French since I was ten. (i.e. since a point in time)

– **among, between**

That family is always quarrelling among themselves. (i.e. a number of people)

She stood between her mother and father. (i.e. only two people)

– **as, like**

You're as daft as a brush. (i.e. 'as' is a preposition)

I soon stopped swimming as the water was so cold. (i.e. 'as' is a conjunction)

Like a fool, I gave him my money. (i.e. 'like' is a preposition)

BUT John cannot bowl like his brother can. (i.e. 'like' is not a conjunction and correct usage should be: 'John cannot bowl *as* his brother can.')

■ **Compound prepositions consist of more than one word.** The most common are:

according to	as well as	by means of
by way of	except for	in addition to
in aid of	in front of	in place of
instead of	next to	on account of
out of	owing to	with regard to

Skills practice: *using prepositions*

Exercise A
Copy out these sentences and highlight or underline all the prepositions. Check back to the examples if you need to.

1 He will probably arrive by six o'clock.

2 I will meet you there at five-thirty.

3 We have lived in the north for three years.

4 On February 8th I shall be 21.

5 What on earth is that under the table?

6 She divided the cake among her five children.

7 Mr Watts was standing in the field when the storm broke.

8 Richard had waited over half an hour at the corner of the street.

9 She leaned towards me and whispered in my ear.

10 An old man with a scruffy beard peered out of the window.

Exercise B
Copy out these sentences, completing them with an appropriate preposition. Look at the examples again, for help.

1 Swallows gather to migrate _____ the autumn.

2 We have had no rain now _____ three months.

3 The party should be over _____ 11 o'clock.

4 Jane and Zoe should arrive _____ any minute.

5 He has limped on that leg _____ childhood.

6 Grandma hung the new calendar _____ the mantelpiece.

7 We could see the airport spread out _____ us.

8 I shall fight _____ that proposal until my dying day.

9 He's always falling _____ his bike.

10 The railway line runs _____ the river and the motorway.

Exercise C

Copy out and complete these sentences with a compound preposition. Check back to the examples, if you need to.

1. _____ this book, the buried treasure was found in the old well.
2. There's a hot dog stall _____ the stadium.
3. The sale was held _____ disabled children.
4. Lee played _____ Martin, who didn't turn up.
5. Everyone contributed something _____ old Scrooge over there.
6. I was standing _____ the fire alarm when it went off.
7. _____ your plan to pull down the children's playground, we wish to express our opposition.
8. Tim passed his exams _____ playing for the football team.
9. The rugby ground is _____ the cricket ground.
10. Lesley accepted the award _____ of Carol, who was in America.

Word building: *prefixes*

So far, much of the work you have done on word building has focused on suffixes or word endings.

A prefix is a group of letters added to the beginning of a word stem, often to create its opposite meaning.

Adding a prefix to a word is usually more straightforward than adding a suffix: neither the spelling of the stem nor the spelling of the prefix changes so frequently.

For example: '**un–**' joins onto 'necessary' to form 'unnecessary'

> *(Notice that the spelling of the root word and the prefix do not change, so there is a double 'n' at the beginning – unnecessary.)*

> '**under**' joins onto 'ground' to form 'underground'

1 Negative prefixes – form words opposite in meaning to the root word. The most common ones are:

'**un–**', '**dis–**', '**ir–**', '**im–**', '**in–**', '**il–**'.

For example: un + acceptable   unacceptable

            dis + similar   dissimilar

            ir + relevant   irrelevant

            im + patient   impatient

            in + efficient   inefficient

            il + legal   illegal

2 'mis–' is slightly different; it may be added to past participles to indicate that the action has been incorrectly or inadequately performed.

For example: 'Misdirected' means you were given the wrong directions, not that you were given none.

'Misinformed' means you were given some information but it was wrong; 'uninformed' means you were given no information.

3 Two prefixes that do change their spelling are 'all' and 'well'. When these are added to a word stem, the second 'l' is dropped.

For example: all + most   almost

            all + so   also

            all + mighty   almighty

            all + ready   already

            all + together   altogether

            all + ways   always

            well + come   welcome

            well + fare   welfare

4 Adverbs may be used as prefixes. Nouns, verbs and adjectives are sometimes created by adding an adverb as a prefix to the word stem.

For example: out + let   an outlet

over + throw	to overthrow
up + set	an upset **or** to upset
down + hearted	downhearted

5 **The prefixes 'be–' and 'en–/m–', meaning 'to make' or 'create a state of', are sometimes added to nouns and adjectives to create verbs.**

For example:	be + witch	to bewitch
	en + large	to enlarge
	em + bitter	to embitter

6 **The prefix 're–' with a hyphen may be added to almost any verb to describe a repetition of the action.**

| For example: | re– + read | to re-read (to read again) |
| | re– + enter | to re-enter (to enter again) |

(Note: in some words, the prefix 're' has been absorbed into the word, e.g. reduce, respond, release, relax. In these cases the original meaning of the prefix has changed or been lost.)

Skills practice: *adding prefixes*

Exercise A
Complete this table by adding the negative prefixes in– or ir–, as appropriate. The first one has been done for you as an example.

Word	Negative form
defensible	*indefensible*
dependent	
rational	
resistible	
eligible	
digestible	
responsible	
definable	
regular	
famous	
reversible	

Exercise B

Complete this table by adding the negative prefixes, il– or im–, as appropriate. The first one has been done for you as an example.

Word	Negative form
mature	*immature*
modest	
logical	
perfect	
legitimate	
possible	
moral	
legible	
proper	
prudent	
literate	

Exercise C

Complete this table by adding the negative prefixes un–, dis– or mis–, as appropriate. The first one has been done for you as an example.

Word	Negative form
desirable	*undesirable*
certain	
orderly	
laid	
continued	
workable	
trust*	
agree	
led	
favourable	
satisfied	

(Note: this one has two negative forms!)

Exercise D

Complete this table by using the adverbs 'up', 'down', 'out' and 'in', as appropriate, as prefixes to complete the words. The first one has been done for you as an example.

Word	New word
–bringing	upbringing
–cast	
–put	
–pour	
–roar	
–break	
–come	
–cry	
–right	
–keep	
–burst	

Exercise E

Complete this table by using the adverbs 'over', 'under', 'off' and 'on', as appropriate, as prefixes to complete the words. The first one has been done for you as an example.

Word	New word
–flow	overflow
–wear	
–hang	
–set	
–looker	
–take	
–line	
–spring	
–rush	
–look	
–come	

Exercise F

Complete this table by using the prefixes be– and en–/m–, as appropriate, to complete the words. The first one has been done for you as an example.

Word	Verb
danger	*endanger*
slave	
trust	
courage	
friend	
siege	
sure	
large	
moan	
joy	
calm	

Text building: *openings*

In the last unit, you learned about organising your writing in a clear and interesting way, using paragraphs to help your reader understand precisely what you have to say.

However, none of this will matter if you don't produce an interesting opening to your writing, because no one will bother to read more than a few sentences.

Probably the most famous openings are:

> 'In the beginning, God created the Heaven and the Earth.' (*The Bible*)

> 'Once upon a time …' (traditional fairy stories)

■ **You need to find something more original. Your opening must excite the reader's interest.**

1 Narrative writing ('stories')

Your opening may:

■ pose a problem – which the reader will want to know the solution to.

'Hale knew, before he had been in Brighton three hours, that they meant to murder him.'

(*Brighton Rock* by Graham Greene)

■ suggest an unusual development in a normal situation.

'Before she came to Belton, Minty Cane had known that she was a witch, or something very like it.'

(*Moondial* by Helen Cresswell)

■ use humour to engage the reader.

'Describe, using diagrams where appropriate, the exact circumstances leading to your death.'

(*Red Dwarf – Infinity Welcomes Careful Drivers* by Grant Naylor)

■ cut into a piece of dialogue so the reader wants to know who is talking about whom.

'They were driving into Garmouth before Mother said defensively:

"You do remember Prudie, don't you?"

"Course I remember Prudie," snapped Anne. "She did look after me till I was eight." '

(*The Watch House* by Robert Westall)

■ start with a slightly surprising general statement which the writer clearly intends to prove.

'All happy families are alike but an unhappy family is unhappy after its own fashion.' (*Anna Karenina* by Leo Tolstoy)

2 Non-narrative writing (discussions, reports, etc.)

Your opening could be:

■ a proposition (a general statement) you set out to prove by using argument and examples.

'We are capable of seeing only what we want to see.'

('The Appearance of Reality' in *Paperweight* by Stephen Fry)

■ an obvious fact presented in an arresting way.

'When the Queen picks up her cracker this Christmas she, like the rest of us, won't have a clue what it contains.'

(The beginning of an article about someone who makes Christmas crackers by Mike Ward, *The Express on Sunday* Magazine, 14 December 1997.)

■ an unusual circumstance associated with the subject.

'It's improbable but entirely appropriate that Peter and I should have been introduced to each other by a bishop.'

(The beginning of a tribute to Peter Cook by Nicholas Luard, in 'The Man Who Lit a Bonfire' in *Peter Cook Remembered*, edited by Lin Cook.)

■ *Remember, before you begin writing – having thought through your material and how you are going to organise it – spend some time creating a really good opening sentence.*

■ *Make sure it is relevant and appropriate to what follows.*

Skills practice: *openings*

Write an opening sentence to each of the following:

1 a story suitable for children aged 7–10;

2 a report for your class newspaper of an interview with the school 'lollipop' person;

3 a mystery story set in your local bus station;

4 a description of the school playing field in January;

5 an account of things that annoy you.

Writing

■ Take the best of your 'openings' and develop it into a finished piece of work.

■ You will need to spend some time planning how the writing will develop beyond the initial stage you thought up for the last section.

Unit 17: Better endings

In this unit you will:

- read an extract from an African novel;
- learn about comparatives and superlatives;
- learn more about prefixes;
- learn about and practise ending written work effectively.

Speaking and listening

- You and a partner are to make a presentation to the rest of the class.

- Choose a topic you know a lot about and plan what you think would make an interesting 4–5 minute presentation.

- Make notes; decide which of you will deal with which aspects of the topic; practise quietly together.

- Give your talk to the class as part of the portfolio of oral activities that will form the basis of your end of key stage assessment.

Understanding

You have looked at the presentation of character through dialogue in previous units. Think about the impression you are given of Okonkwo and his father, Unoka, in this opening passage from *Things Fall Apart* by Chinua Achebe, and then answer the question that follows.

> Okonkwo was well known throughout the nine villages and even beyond. His fame rested on solid personal achievements. As a young man of eighteen he had brought honour to his village by throwing Amalinze the Cat. Amalinze was the great wrestler who
> 5 for seven years was unbeaten, from Umuofia to Mbaino. He was called the Cat because his back would never touch the earth. It was this man that Okonkwo threw in a fight which the old men agreed was one of the fiercest since the founder of their town

continued …

engaged a spirit of the wild for seven days and seven nights.

10   The drums beat and the flutes sang and the spectators held their breath. Amalinze was a wily craftsman, but Okonkwo was as slippery as a fish in water. Every nerve and every muscle stood out on their arms, on their backs and their thighs, and one almost heard them stretching to breaking point. In the end Okonkwo
15 threw the Cat.

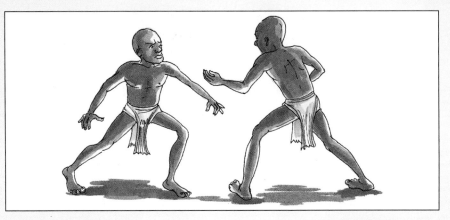

    That was many years ago, twenty years or more, and during this time Okonkwo's fame had grown like a bushfire in the harmattan. He was tall and huge, and his bushy eyebrows and wide nose gave him a very severe look. He breathed heavily, and
20 it was said that when he slept, his wives and children in their outhouses could hear him breathe. When he walked, his heels hardly touched the ground and he seemed to walk on springs, as if he was going to pounce on somebody. And he did pounce on people quite often. He had a slight stammer and whenever he was
25 angry and could not get his words out quickly enough, he would use his fists. He had no patience with unsuccessful men. He had had no patience with his father.

    Unoka, for that was his father's name, had died ten years ago. In his day he was lazy and improvident and was quite incapable
30 of thinking about tomorrow. If any money came his way, and it seldom did, he immediately bought gourds of palm wine, called

round his neighbours and made merry. He always said that whenever he saw a dead man's mouth he saw the folly of not eating what one had in one's lifetime. Unoka was, of course, a
35 debtor, and he owed every neighbour some money, from a few cowries to quite substantial amounts.

   He was tall but very thin and had a slight stoop. He wore a haggard and mournful look except when he was drinking or playing on his flute. He was very good on his flute, and his
40 happiest moments were the two or three moons after the harvest when the village musicians brought down their instruments, hung above the fireplace. Unoka would play with them, his face beaming with blessedness and peace. Sometimes another village would ask Unoka's band and their dancing egwugwu to come
45 and stay with them and teach them their tunes. They would go to such hosts for as long as three or four markets, making music and feasting. Unoka loved the good fare and the good fellowship, and he loved this season of the year, when the rains had stopped and the sun rose every morning with dazzling beauty. And it was not
50 too hot either, because the cold and dry harmattan wind was blowing down from the north. Some years the harmattan was very severe and a dense haze hung on the atmosphere. Old men and children would then sit round log fires, warming their bodies.

   Unoka loved it all, and he loved
55 the kites that returned with the dry season, and the children who sang songs of welcome to them. He would remember his own childhood, how he had often
60 wandered around looking for a kite sailing leisurely against the blue sky. As soon as he found one he would sing with his whole

continued …

being, welcoming it back from its long, long journey, and asking it
65 if it had brought home any lengths of cloth.

That was years ago, when he was young. Unoka, the grown-up, was a failure. He was poor and his wife and children had barely enough to eat. People laughed at him because he was a loafer, and they swore never to lend him any more money because he never
70 paid back. But Unoka was such a man that he always succeeded in borrowing more, and piling up his debts.

When Unoka died he had taken no title at all and he was heavily in debt. Any wonder then that his son Okonkwo was ashamed of him? Fortunately, among these people a man was
75 judged according to his worth and not according to the worth of his father. Okonkwo was clearly cut out for great things. He was still young but he had won fame as the greatest wrestler in the nine villages. He was a wealthy farmer and had two barns full of yams, and had just married his third wife. To crown it all he had
80 taken two titles and had shown incredible prowess in two inter-tribal wars. And so although Okonkwo was still young, he was already one of the greatest men of his time. Age was respected among his people, but achievement was revered.

Now answer this question:

In what ways are Okonkwo and his father, Unoka, presented differently in this opening passage of the book?

You should comment on:

- their achievements;
- their hopes and ambitions;
- their attitudes to life;
- the way they are seen by others in the tribe.

Look carefully at what each character says and does and the language used to describe them. Use this evidence from the text to support your comments.

Learning about language: *comparatives and superlatives*

The comparative and superlative forms of adjectives and adverbs are used when a comparison is made between the qualities of two or more things or actions.

For example: 'I am wiser than you' makes a comparison between the wisdom of just two people – 'I' and 'you' – and decides whose is greater. This is the **comparative form**: 'wiser' is a **comparative adjective**.

'I am the wisest in the class' makes a comparison between the wisdom of more than one other person – 'I' and 'the rest of the class' – and decides mine is the greatest. This is the **superlative form**: 'wisest' is a **superlative adjective**.

'I was injured more seriously than you' compares the extent of my injuries with yours and decides who suffered more (only two people). This is the **comparative form**: 'more seriously' is a **comparative adverb**.

'I was the most seriously injured' compares the extent of my injuries with those of more than one other person (all those who were injured) and decides who suffered the most. This is the **superlative form**: 'most seriously' is a **superlative adverb**.

1 The comparative form of adjectives – when only two items are compared – is created by adding the suffix '-er'; and the superlative form – when more than two items are compared – by adding the suffix '-est' to:

■ all adjectives of only one syllable:
e.g. longer, shortest

■ adjectives of two syllables ending in '-ow', '-y', '-le' and '-er':
e.g. hollower, ugliest (remember the final '-y' spelling rule), simpler (remember the final '-e' spelling rule), cleverest

■ adjectives of two syllables with the accent on the first syllable:
e.g. quieter, wickedest

(These adjectives may also use 'more' and 'most' instead of the suffixes: e.g. more quiet, most wicked.)

2 All other adjectives form the comparative and the superlative by using 'more' and 'most':

e.g. more difficult, most capable

3 The comparative and superlative of adverbs is formed using the suffixes '-er' and '-est' for single syllable adverbs:

e.g. harder, highest

4 Adverbs of two or more syllables form the comparative and superlative using 'more' and 'most':

e.g. more quickly, most successfully

5 The following forms are irregular:

Positive	Comparative	Superlative
well	better	best
badly	worse	worst
little	less	least
much	more	most
far	farther*	farthest*

(* *Usually spelt further/furthest.*)

Skills practice: *forming and using comparatives and superlatives*

Exercise A
Complete this table with the comparative form of the adjectives and adverbs given. The first one has been done for you as an example.

Positive	Comparative
young	*younger*
humble	
rainy	

ugly	
beautiful	
true	
harmlessly	
soon	
yellow	
guilty	
evil	
childish	
near	
kindly	
rapid	
much	
interestingly	
likely	
modest	
sunny	
politely	

Exercise B
Complete this table with the superlative form of the adjectives and adverbs given. The first one has been done for you as an example.

Positive	Superlative
warm	*warmest*
gentle	
worthy	
easy	
wonderful	
blue	
thoughtless	
even	
contentedly	
angry	
cruel	
foolish	

continued ...

far	
lovely	
fierce	
little	
surprisingly	
elderly	
thorough	
silly	
shallow	

Exercise C

Copy out this passage and complete it by filling the spaces with the comparative or superlative form of appropriate adjectives or adverbs. You may choose words that make the passage amusing provided your choice makes sense!

Our class must be the _____ in the country. You will never meet a _____ group of people. Our teacher, Mrs Andrews, is the _____ in the school – and so tall, she must be _____ than the M1! Of all the boys, Damian must be the _____ but Natalie Mills is even _____ than him. That pair should apply to the 'Guinness Book of Records' to become the _____ idiots of all time! At the other extreme, Shireen, the _____ person in the class, is going to take her GCSEs a year early. She's expected to get the _____ results in the school.

Lessons seem to become _____ every day. In English all we do is read a textbook. Can you imagine anything _____ ? Yesterday, though, we had the _____ lessons ever. In chemistry, Sharon set fire to her hair with the Bunsen burner. I've never heard anyone scream _____ . Then in biology, Nathan fainted during a dissection. It was probably the _____ day of his life – I have never seen anything _____ . What could be _____ than that?

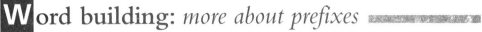

Word building: *more about prefixes*

In the Unit 15 exercise on '-ology' words, you learned that many English words have Latin or Greek origins. Prefixes, especially, seem to have their origins in these classical languages and some are listed, with their meanings, in the following tables.

From Latin

Prefix	Meaning	Example
ante–	before	antenatal
bi–/bis–	two	biannual
circum–	around	circumference
con–	with	conform
contra–	against	contraflow
dis–	put aside	disprove
e–/ex–	out of	expel
in–	not	inexpensive
inter–	among/between	interconnecting
mis–	badly	misguided
multi–	many	multilateral
post–	after	postscript
pre–	before	prejudge
pro–	supporting	pro-democracy
quad–	four	quadrangle
re–	back/again	repay
semi–	half	semi-skilled
sub–	under	submarine
super–	over	supersonic
trans–	across	transfusion

From Greek

Prefix	Meaning	Example
a–/ab–	without	amoral
ambi–/amphi–	both sides	amphibian
anti–	against	antibody
auto–	self	autopilot
hyper–	excessive	hypersensitive
mono–	single/alone	monochrome
poly–	many	polygon
pseudo–	false	pseudonym
tele–	distant	telephone
tri–	three	tricycle

Skills practice: *word formation with prefixes*

Exercise A

Complete this table by adding appropriate prefixes of Latin origin to the words given. The first one has been done for you as an example.

Word	New word
use	disuse
stance	
change	
diction	
parent	
chamber	
caution	
text	
centenary	
miss	
coloured	
face	
graduate	

discipline	
European	
take	
final	
lapse	
merge	
–raphonic	
human	

Exercise B

Complete this table by adding appropriate prefixes of Greek origin to the words given. The first one has been done for you as an example.

Word	New word
plane	*monoplane*
matter	
void	
tone	
syllabic	
active	
intellectual	
vision	
biography	
angle	
dextrous	

Text building: *endings*

- In the last unit, you learned about 'opening' your piece of writing in a clear and interesting way.

- It is just as important to bring your work to an effective conclusion, leaving the reader with a sense of 'completeness' and a clear idea of where the journey through your work has ended.

- In narrative writing (a story), situations may need to be resolved, in some cases, perhaps, by things simply carrying on unchanged or returning to 'normal'; in non-narrative writing (reports, discussions), by a sense that a point has been made, an argument proved or an explanation given.

Probably the most famous ending is:

'… and they all lived happily ever after.' (traditional fairy stories)

Pupils often simply end:

'And then I woke up and realised it was all a dream!'

As with openings, you need to find something original. You must leave your reader feeling that the 'journey' has been completed and that they know the destination they have arrived at.

1 Narrative writing (stories)

Your ending may be:

- the main character or characters dying/'moving on' to something different/a new life:

  'He turned the ignition and smiled as the Cavalier trembled to life. He put the car into gear. He knew he could never go back.'

  (Percy leaving Gorleston in Henry Sutton's *Gorleston*)

- a tribute to the main character who has died or 'moved on':

  '… him whom I shall ever regard as the best and wisest man whom I have ever known.'

  (Dr Watson's tribute to Sherlock Holmes at the end of 'The Final Problem' in Conan Doyle's *Memoirs of Sherlock Holmes*)

- a piece of dialogue/concluding statement/final words from a central character:

  ' "It is a far, far better thing that I do, than I have ever done; it is a far, far better rest that I go to than I have ever known." '

  (The words of Sydney Carton as he goes to the guillotine at the end of Dickens' *A Tale of Two Cities*)

- something humorous to 'get the writer off the hook' or an indication that the whole thing was 'only a story':

  'There was a point to this story, but it has temporarily escaped the chronicler's mind.'

  (Douglas Adams' ending of 'So Long and Thanks for all the Fish' in *The Hitchhiker's Guide to the Galaxy*)

'Then the Queen said,

"I think we ought to get the book printed properly and published so that other children can read it."

This was arranged, but because the BFG was a very modest giant, he wouldn't put his own name to it. He used somebody else's name instead.

But where, you might ask, is this book that the BFG wrote? It's right here. You've just finished reading it.'

(Roald Dahl's ending of *The BFG*)

'Come, children, let us shut the box and the puppets, for our play is played out.'

(William Thackeray's ending of *Vanity Fair*)

■ a slightly surprising general statement, the truth of which has been 'proved' by what has happened:

'And it may be that love sometimes occurs without pain or misery'.

(E. Annie Proulx's ending of *The Shipping News*)

2 Non-narrative writing (discussions, reports etc.)

Your ending could be:

■ the subject has been fully explored or the proposition/point proved:

'The tide was high. I started down the long pier towards the shore, trying to figure out a way of getting home.'

(Paul Theroux at Southend at the end of his round tour of Britain in *The Kingdom by the Sea*)

■ the investigation/discussion continues:

'… we shall all … be able to take part in the discussion of the question of why it is that we and the universe exist. If we find the answer to that, it would be the ultimate triumph of human reason − for then we would know the mind of God.'

(Stephen Hawking's *A Brief History of Time*)

■ an appropriate – and possibly witty – quotation:

'It was such sheer unmatched comfort that prompted Spencer Tracy to say: "Not that I intend to die, but when I do, I don't want to go to heaven, I want to go to Claridge's."'

(The ending to an article about Claridge's Hotel by Marcus Binney in *The Times* Magazine of 20 December 1997)

Having planned your writing, thought through your material and how you are going to organise it, finally spend some time creating an effective and appropriate ending.

Skills practice: *endings*

Write the last three or four sentences to each of the following:

■ your autobiography;

■ a science fiction story ending with the first person to land on Mars meeting … ;

■ a letter home from a soldier expecting to go into battle the next day;

■ a story for 5–7 year olds;

■ a report for your school magazine on the work of the School Council;

■ a story set in an ordinary school/family which ends on the day the GCSE results are published.

Writing

■ Look back through your folder of work and select three pieces of writing where you think you could improve the endings.

■ Rewrite the last paragraph of each and attach it to the original for consideration at your end of key stage assessment of written work.

Unit 18: Writing letters

In this unit you will:

- read three different letters;
- learn about correctness and accuracy in your writing;
- learn about hyphens and compound words;
- learn about and practise writing letters.

Speaking and listening

Working with a partner, read through the three letters in the next section of this unit. Make notes on:

- the purpose of each letter;
- how this affects the different tone of each letter;
- how the tone is achieved by the use of verbs – tense, mood and voice;
- any other features of the language used in one letter which is different from the other two.

Understanding

Three letters follow:

- a letter from WWF–UK seeking new members;
- a letter from Helen to her sister at the beginning of E.M. Forster's *Howards End*;
- a letter of complaint from a dissatisfied customer.

There are occasions when you will be expected to write or speak in a more formal way than usual. Common examples of 'formal communication' involve writing letters of application for jobs and speaking at job interviews. Being formal means adopting an appropriately serious and sensible tone and following agreed rules of behaviour. In practical terms, this requires the use of standard English and the avoidance of slang or 'chatty' language. This section focuses on the different language requirements of formal and informal letters. You have already read the letters through and discussed them with your partner. Now read the letters again and then complete the task that follows.

WWF-UK,

Panda House, Weyside Park,

Godalming, Surrey GU7 1XR.

Telephone: (01483) 426444

Fax: (01483) 426409

G66G/050163369

Mr D.A. Jackson,

27 Bondgate Street,

Manchester.

15th May 1997

Dear Mr Jackson,

As you probably know, it has been some time now since your WWF membership expired and I am writing to ask you to consider joining us once again.

I appreciate, of course, that your priorities and commitments may have changed since you originally joined, but did you realise that you can renew your membership for as little as £2 per month? That, alone, would help pay for a walkie-talkie that anti-poaching rangers use when patrolling National Parks. Believe me, every penny helps.

But the money isn't the only reason we need you. The truth is that, without you, we're weaker – and the weaker we are, the less influence we have. And we need that influence as much today as ever before.

Without the support of our members, we simply wouldn't have the money to protect endangered species as we have in Nepal's National Parks, for example, where *not one* tiger or rhino has been poached since 1994! Or the leverage to establish important conservation initiatives like the Marine Stewardship Council which will work to combat the destruction of ocean ecosystems through overfishing. But, even more importantly, we would not have had the *authority* to negotiate at a global level without the mandate of over 5 million supporters world-wide. That's why *your* support is so important.

Each step we take is one step nearer to a safer world, a cleaner world, in which our natural heritage is protected against wasteful neglect and destruction – and we need you with us.

Can you imagine having to show your grandchildren a photograph of an elephant or rhino and explain how these magnificent creatures were wiped out simply because it just wasn't important enough?

The truth is that, without WWF, there is a very real possibility that these animals would now already be extinct.

You once cared enough to support our work – I'm asking you now to remember why you joined us and to join us once again.

You'll see that, at the bottom of your membership renewal application, there's a Direct Debit form. You can use it to spread the cost of your membership, making monthly payments.

However you choose to rejoin, the main thing for us is to have you back as one of our supporters.

So, please, do spare a few moments to consider the importance of our work. All you need do is complete the renewal form and return it to us in the envelope provided.

Thank you.

Robin Pellew

Robin Pellew
Director, WWF-UK

Howards End

Tuesday

Dearest Meg,

It isn't going to be what we expected. It is old and little, and
altogether delightful – red brick. We can scarcely pack in as it is,
and the dear knows what will happen when Paul (younger son)
arrives tomorrow. From hall you go right or left into dining-room
or drawing room. Hall itself is practically a room. You open
another door in it, and there are the stairs going up in a sort of
tunnel to the first-floor. Three bedrooms in a row there, and three
attics in a row above. That isn't all the house really, but it's all that
one notices – nine windows as you look up from the front garden.

Then there's a very big wych-elm – to the left as you look up –
leaning a little over the house, and standing on the boundary
between the garden and meadow. I quite love that tree already.
Also ordinary elms, oaks – no nastier than ordinary oaks – pear-
trees, apple-trees, and a vine. No silver birches, though. However,
I must get on to my host and hostess. I only wanted to show that it
isn't the least what we expected. Why did we settle that their
house would be all gables and wiggles, and their garden all
gamboge-coloured paths? I believe simply because we associate
them with expensive hotels – Mrs Wilcox trailing in beautiful
dresses down long corridors, Mr Wilcox bullying porters, etc. We
females are that unjust.

I shall be back Saturday; will let you know train later. They are
as angry as I am that you did not come too; really Tibby is too
tiresome, he starts a new mortal disease every month. How could
he have got hay fever in London? and even if he could, it seems
hard that you should give up a visit to hear a schoolboy sneeze.
Tell him that Charles Wilcox (the son who is here) has hay fever
too, but he's brave, and gets quite cross when we inquire after it.
Men like the Wilcoxes would do Tibby a power of good. But you
won't agree, and I'd better change the subject.

This long letter is because I'm writing before breakfast. Oh, the
beautiful vine leaves! The house is covered with a vine. I looked
out earlier, and Mrs Wilcox was already in the garden. She
evidently loves it. No wonder she sometimes looks tired. She was

watching the large red poppies come out. Then she walked off the lawn to the meadow, whose corner to the right I can just see. Trail, trail, went her long dress over the sopping grass, and she came back with her hands full of the hay that was cut yesterday – I suppose for rabbits or something, as she kept on smelling it. The air here is delicious. Later on I heard the noise of croquet balls, and looked out again, and it was Charles Wilcox practising; they are keen on all games. Presently he started sneezing and had to stop. Then I hear more clicketing, and it is Mr Wilcox practising, and the, 'a-tishoo, a-tishoo': he has to stop too. Then Evie comes out, and does come calisthenic exercises on a machine that is tacked on to a greengage-tree – they put everything to use – and then she says ' a-tishoo,' and in she goes. And finally Mrs Wilcox reappears, trail, trail, still smelling hay and looking at the flowers. I inflict all this on you because once you said that life is sometimes life and sometimes only a drama, and one must learn to distinguish tother from which, and up to now I have always put that down as 'Meg's clever nonsense.' But this morning, it really does seem not life but a play, and it did amuse me enormously to watch the W's. Now Mrs Wilcox has come in.

I am going to wear (omission). Last night Mrs Wilcox wore an (omission), and Evie (omission). So it isn't exactly a go-as-you-please place, and if you shut your eyes it still seems the wiggly hotel that we expected. Not if you open them. The dog-roses are too sweet. There is a great hedge of them over the lawn – magnificently tall, so that they fall down in garlands, and nice and thin at the bottom, so that you can see ducks through it and a cow. These belong to the farm, which is the only house near us. There goes the breakfast gong. Much love. Modified love to Tibby. Love to Aunt Juley; how good of her to come and keep you company, but what a bore. Burn this. Will write again Thursday.

Helen

The Managing Director,   David Johnson,
Black and White Garage,   14 Swan Way,
Maidenhead Road,   Slough,
Slough,   Berkshire.
Berkshire.

12th October 1997

Dear Sir,

<u>Re: servicing of my car, BMW 318 series</u>

I collected my car yesterday morning after it had been in your service department for the whole week, having a full service and having all the battery/electric systems checked. This was because short-circuiting or some other cause was draining power from the battery, leaving it totally flat after a very short period.

I was informed that the problem was the alternator and a new one was fitted at a cost of over £200.

When I collected the car yesterday I was a little surprised to be told that the battery was still a 'bit flat' but a 'good run' should sort it out.

I took the car for a 'good run' down the M4 to Maidenhead and my wife and I spent about an hour shopping and having afternoon tea. I returned to the car to drive home – the battery was totally flat and, of course, I couldn't start the engine to get home without having to call out assistance.

In short, the major problem which had put my car off the road had not been properly diagnosed and dealt with. The fact that your service managers had some trouble getting it started yesterday morning when I came to collect it might have alerted them to the fact that the problem had not been cured.

I certainly felt more than a little annoyed yesterday afternoon when within four hours of paying your company £770, I found myself with a car that wouldn't go!

I suspect you might wish to institute a rigorous review of your service department's performance, but in the meantime I look forward to any suggestions you might have about getting my car properly checked, repaired and back on the road.

Yours faithfully,

David Johnson

David Johnson

Using the notes you compiled with your partner at the beginning of this unit, write a detailed account of how each letter uses language differently to achieve its purpose.

You should

- explain the purpose and intention of each letter
- comment on how these influence the tone of the letter
- show how choice of vocabulary, choice of verb forms and structure of sentences contribute to these differences of tone.

Learning about language: *concord (agreement), ambiguity and redundancy*

These three terms refer to aspects of written language where mistakes often occur.

- **Concord or agreement refers to the need for each word in a sentence to agree grammatically with the other words in the sentence.**

1 **Beware of repeating mistakes from careless spoken language: the verb form must always be the appropriate one – i.e. 'agree with' – the subject.**

For example: 'We was robbed' is incorrect. 'We' is a plural subject but 'was' is a singular verb.

2 **Beware of complex subjects in a sentence – the subject and verb form must still agree.**

For example: 'The last of the dangers were the three-headed dragon' is incorrect. 'The last' is a single object and 'were' is a plural verb form; only one danger is referred to.

BUT 'She is one of those girls who enjoys making trouble' is incorrect. The subject of 'enjoys' is 'those girls who', which is plural; 'enjoys' is a singular form.

3 Beware of collective nouns as subjects; they usually need a singular verb form.

For example: 'The class were not paying attention' is incorrect. 'The class' is a single item but 'were not paying' is a plural verb form.

4 Beware of sentences where a phrase comes between the subject and the verb – they must still agree.

For example: 'My father, with his younger brother, were flying out in the morning' is incorrect. 'My father' (singular) is the subject of the main clause; 'were flying' is a plural verb form.

5 Beware of pronouns such as 'everyone', 'everybody', 'no one' and 'nobody' (including 'none'), which usually require a singular verb form.

For example: 'Nobody were laughing at his performance' is incorrect. 'Were laughing' is a plural verb form.

'None of these explanations are acceptable' is incorrect. 'None' means 'not one'(singular) and 'are' is a plural verb form.

6 Beware of 'either … or' and 'neither … nor' which require a singular verb form if the individual alternatives are singular, but a plural verb form if one of the alternatives is plural.

For example: 'Either Helen or Jane are responsible' is incorrect, as both of the alternatives – 'Helen' and 'Jane' – are singular, but 'are' is a plural verb form.

BUT 'Neither Helen nor the other girls is responsible' is incorrect because one of the alternatives – 'the other girls' – is plural and 'is' is a singular verb form.

■ **Ambiguity refers to sentences that have more than one interpretation. If the ambiguity is unintentional, the meaning is not clear.**

1 **Beware of not linking or relating participles to the correct item.**

For example: 'Living in the north, the sun rarely shines on us in winter' suggests that either 'we' or 'the sun' lives in the north. Ambiguity is avoided by: 'As we live in the north, the sun rarely shines on us in winter.'

2 **Beware of careless word order; make sure that a qualifying phrase or clause is placed next to the word it relates to.**

For example: 'Wanted: bath for baby with tin bottom.' This suggests that either the baby or the bath could have the 'tin bottom'.

Ambiguity is avoided by: 'Wanted: bath with tin bottom for baby.'

3 **Beware of using 'only'; make sure it refers to the right word and that other important words are not left out.**

For example: 'Only trainers are to be worn in the gym' suggests that either 'trainers are the only form of footwear allowed' or that 'trainers and nothing else are to be worn'.

Ambiguity is avoided by: 'Trainers are the only footwear to be worn in the gym.'

4 **Beware of pronouns that are not clearly related to the correct object or person.**

For example: 'I took my dirty washing out of the suitcase and threw it into the washing machine' does not make it clear whether it was the washing or the suitcase that went into the washing machine.

Ambiguity is avoided by: 'I threw the dirty washing, which I had taken out of my suitcase, into the washing machine.'

■ **Redundancy refers to the use of unnecessary words that add no further meaning to a sentence.**

For example: 'They called the three triplets Sophie, Bianca and Shelley'. 'Three' adds nothing to the meaning because 'triplets' means 'a group of three'. The sentence is better expressed by leaving out 'three'.

'Everyone present unanimously agreed that she should resign.' 'Unanimously' means 'everyone'. The sentence is better expressed by leaving out 'unanimously' or as 'It was unanimously agreed …'

■ **A particular form of redundancy is the use of the 'double negative' – often picked up from spoken language.**

For example: 'I didn't do nothing!' This suggests that the speaker did not 'do nothing' and, therefore, must have 'done something'.

Preferable forms are: 'I did nothing' or 'I didn't do anything.'

Skills practice: *checking for agreement, ambiguity and redundancy*

Exercise A
Copy out these sentences and complete them with the correct verb form – singular or plural – which agrees with the subject. (In some cases you may use either the present or past tense form.) Check back to the examples if you need to.

1 There _____ plenty of animals to look at in the zoo.

2 Simon and Becky both _____ musical instruments.

3 The girls _____ a netball match this afternoon.

4 My sister and her friend _____ going to India for six weeks.

5 My sister, with her pet dog, _____ walking slowly across the road.

6 The pack of cards _____ in the cupboard.

7 The first of my presents _____ a new computer game.

8 Danny is one of those boys who _____ at anything.

Exercise B

Copy out these sentences and complete them with the correct verb form – singular or plural. (In some cases you may use either the present or the past tense.) Look at the examples again if you need to.

1 No one _____ walking round the city last night.
2 Either John or Edward _____ going away on holiday.
3 Everybody _____ doing homework in the lunch hour, I discovered.
4 Neither Jackie nor Kirsten _____ finished the test.
5 Neither the elephants nor the monkeys _____ very entertaining at the circus.
6 None of these pairs of boots _____ suitable for orienteering.
7 Everyone _____ chatting when the head teacher walked in.
8 Either Shabir or one of the other boys in his group _____ going to write up the report.

Exercise C

Rewrite these sentences to remove any ambiguity caused by unrelated participles or the misplacing of 'only'. Look back at the examples if you need to.

1 Walking down the road, the postbox came into view.
2 You only live once.
3 Looking across the fields is the old church tower.
4 Shut up all day, I felt sorry for that wretched dog.
5 Jumping on the bus, the driver asked me for my fare.
6 Fresh fruit only supplied.
7 Driving along the lane, a flock of sheep blocked our way.
8 Running across the road, the car swerved crazily.

Exercise D

Rewrite these sentences to remove any ambiguity caused by careless word order, omissions or unrelated pronouns. Look at the examples again, if you need to.

1 Delays expected on the motorway until January.
2 When leaving the train, may I remind you to take all your belongings with you.
3 Gavin told Carl that he had won the Lottery.
4 There is a cherry tree in the garden that needs attention.

continued ...

5 The doctor told Stephen he wouldn't feel a thing.

6 When I was young, my mother told me stories like *Little Red Riding Hood*.

7 Julie asked Lesley where she had left her purse.

8 Ian enjoyed burgers more than his friends.

9 Car for sale: only one owner, maroon in colour.

10 Dave told Jamie that he was getting fat.

Exercise E
Rewrite these sentences to remove any redundancy.

1 I never said nothing.

2 Can you return these back to the shop?

3 All fixtures between our two schools have been postponed until some future date.

4 I haven't got no one to talk to.

5 You've not got no right to keep me here!

6 The head teacher announced the new innovation in assembly.

7 You go first and I will follow after.

8 The whole school will collaborate together on this project.

9 I will repay back the loan tomorrow.

10 That should leave you with 20 pence left.

Word building: *compound words and hyphens*

- **Compound words are created when two words are brought together to form a new one.** Such new words are usually nouns or adjectives.

  For example: 'class' + 'room' forms the compound noun 'classroom'

  'hand' + 'made' forms the compound adjective 'hand-made'

- **The hyphen is used in compound adjectives.** These are often made with past participles or indicate measurement.

  For example: hand-knitted   well-watered

  30-centimetre   ten-minute
  (ruler etc.)   (interval etc.)

■ **The hyphen is used in compound nouns if the object is thought of as a compound word.**

For example: drawing-room walking-stick

If the two parts of the compound noun are short and the word is commonly used, it is written as one word.

For example: teapot bathroom

If the two parts of the compound noun are long and it is less commonly used, the two parts are written separately.

For example: history lesson insurance policy

Skills practice: *compound words and hyphens*

Exercise A
Change the phrases and clauses in italics into a compound adjective to describe the subject. Check back to the examples if you need to.

For example:
   A young man *who speaks well*   A well-spoken young man

1 A suit *which has been made by a tailor*
2 Ground *which is covered by snow*
3 A drum *which holds four gallons*
4 A table *lit by candles*
5 A pupil *with a quick wit*
6 A castle *built in the fourteenth century*
7 A chair *which is covered with leather*
8 A journey *of three hundred miles*
9 A young woman *who is well dressed*
10 A youth *with long hair*
11 A spoon *which has been plated with silver*
12 A caravan *drawn by a horse*
13 A plateau *which is swept by the wind*
14 A house *with three storeys*
15 A walk *which takes 20 minutes*

Exercise B

Use these pairs of words, joined by a hyphen where appropriate, to form compound nouns. Look at the examples again if you need to.

1 blue/eyed
2 sauce/pan
3 note/paper
4 house/wife
5 reading/lamp
6 milk/jug
7 tea/spoon

8 waist/coat
9 letter/box
10 camp/bed
11 book/shop
12 hand/writing
13 sitting/room
14 sea/shore

Text building: *letter writing*

Note: most of the guidance in this section concerns formal or business letters. Informal and personal letters (see Helen's letter at the beginning of this unit) are written according to the nature of the writer's relationship with the person to whom they are writing. For these you can make up your own rules.

■ **The important rule in punctuating addresses is to be consistent.**

Traditionally letters had full punctuation in the sender's address at the top right-hand side of the letter and in the receiver's address following that on the left-hand side (see the WWF-UK letter and the letter of complaint at the beginning of this unit). Nowadays the tendency is to omit all punctuation from these, and sometimes printed letter heads carry the sender's address right across the top of the page. Either be completely traditional in layout and punctuation, or omit punctuation altogether; do not mix and match!

■ **Always date your letter clearly under your address.**

This may be useful for future reference.

■ **If you are writing to someone you know only by their title – Director, Personnel Officer etc. – begin your letter 'Dear Sir,' and end your letter 'Yours faithfully'.**

- **If you are writing to someone you know by name, begin 'Dear Mr/Mrs/Miss/Ms [name] and end your letter 'Yours sincerely'.**

- **Always sign your letter** – and if you wish to add Miss/Mrs/Ms do so in brackets after your signature.

- **Keep to the point.** Explain why you are writing, give the facts as clearly as possible and explain what action, if any, is expected.

- **Maintain a polite, formal tone.** However upset you may be, explain calmly and clearly why you are upset and what needs to be done. You need to encourage the recipient to be business-like and polite in dealing with you. Do not make threats – you may not be able to carry them out and you will look foolish.

- **If you are putting forward a point of view or explaining an issue, make sure your ideas and arguments are carefully and logically worked out and expressed** (see Unit 15).

ICT Extra!

Sending an e-mail
You could choose to e-mail a reply to Helen. Before you begin to write, think about how this will be different from a short personal letter.

Skills practice and Writing

Write a reply to each of the three letters at the beginning of this unit.

- Explain to WWF-UK why you have decided to subscribe (or not) to the organisation for another year.

- Imagine you are Helen's sister. Write a short, personal letter reacting – as you think appropriate – to Helen's letter.

- Imagine you are the service manager of the garage. Write to the customer explaining what you will do about his complaint.

Unit 19: Figures of speech

In this unit you will:

- read some newspaper reports;
- learn about figures of speech;
- learn about some more easily confused words;
- learn about and practise writing indirect speech.

Speaking and listening

- This activity needs some preparation. Choose a story or event that is currently receiving extensive media coverage.

- Find four different newspapers – for example, *The Mirror*, *The Express*, *The Daily Telegraph* and *The Times* – and cut out the report from each on your chosen subject.

- Working in groups of four, one person with each newspaper, analyse the way the subject is reported in each paper. Collect the following information for each report:

  - how many column inches the subject is given;

  - how many paragraphs each report contains;

  - the average number of sentences in each paragraph;

  - the average number of words in each sentence;

  - word complexity – the ratio of one syllable to multi-syllable (three or more) words;

  - what – and how many – punctuation marks are used apart from sentence markers, commas, apostrophes and punctuation associated with direct speech.

- Compare results and suggest what this tells you about the different approaches of the four papers.

> **ICT Extra!**
>
> **Creating a database/presenting information**
> Create a database for the information you are collecting for each newspaper and enter your results. Experiment with different ways of presenting this information – pie charts, bar graphs, etc. – and decide which format is the most effective. Experiment further by listing the newspapers in rank order according to different characteristics, for example, column inches or average words per sentence.

Understanding

Write a detailed account of the way the newspaper you analysed deals with the subject. You should discuss:

- the amount of space devoted to the subject;
- the 'attitude' of the paper towards the subject, for example, is it supportive, critical, independent?
- in what ways headlines, sub-headings and presentation contribute to the effectiveness of the report;
- how much use each report makes of polysyllabic words (words of three or more syllables);
- how paragraph length and sentence complexity contribute to the effectiveness of the report;
- how far choice of vocabulary and use of punctuation contribute to the impact of the report;
- what sort of readers might find the report interesting;
- major differences from the other papers' reporting of the same subject;
- your verdict on the way the report is presented.

Learning about language: *similes, metaphors and personification*

Language is mostly used **literally** – i.e. it means exactly what it says – and is sometimes used **figuratively** (or **metaphorically**) – i.e. it expresses meaning in a more picturesque way.

For example: 'He's gone round the bend' in a literal sense means that he has disappeared out of sight beyond the curve in the road. In a figurative sense, it means that he has gone crazy or started behaving in a funny or unusual way.

Language is used literally and figuratively when people communicate. For example, if you make a mistake in your work it might be described as a 'silly mistake' (literal) or a 'glaring error' (figurative). In other words, the error does not actually glare at you, but it's such a bad mistake it seems to be glaring at you!

1 **A simile refers to the comparison of one item with another.** It is usually identified by the use of 'like' or 'as' in bringing the two ideas together. It is used to emphasise some quality about the object described and/or for humorous effect.

For example: 'As thin as a rake' is intended to emphasise the thinness of the person referred to, because a rake is a thin pole.

'As safe as an elephant hanging over a cliff with its tail tied to a daisy' may emphasise the lack of safety, but derives its force from the amusing picture created in the mind's eye.

2 **A metaphor is a descriptive term applied to something that is not literally true.** It is a sort of compressed simile because 'like' or 'as' are not used and one thing is said to be another. Again, the intention is to emphasise some quality and/or to provide humour.

For example: 'The shop is opening another branch' is comparing the shop to a tree that grows additional branches, but is making a direct statement that is not literally true – trees, not shops, have branches.

'That boy is an ass' is comparing the boy to a donkey but is making a direct statement that is obviously not true literally, but is perhaps generating some humour at the boy's expense.

3 **Personification refers to a kind of metaphor in which something not human is said to have some qualities – feelings, attitudes, etc. – of a human being.** Again, the purpose is to emphasise some quality and/or create humour.

For example: 'The birds were chattering in the trees' is comparing the birds to humans who 'chatter'; birds do not do so.

For example:

'The Old Lady of Threadneedle Street'
is used to describe the Bank of England,
comparing it to an old woman who presides
over financial affairs.

Skills practice: *recognising similes, metaphors and personification*

Exercise A

Write a short comment on each of these sentences saying whether each contains an example of simile, metaphor or personification. Explain what things are being compared and the effect of the comparison. Look back to the examples if you need to.

1 He could see the great ball of Saturn, surrounded by its rings like a prize on a hoopla stall at a fair.

2 'Break his heart,' Miss Havisham cried.

3 'O! I am Fortune's fool.'

4 The great tragedy of science – the slaying of a beautiful hypothesis by an ugly fact.

5 The future beckoned to me with a smile.

6 That girl is a cabbage.

7 He's as crafty as a fox.

8 Professor Orme is doing research in the field of immunology.

9 The classroom looked as if it had been freshly burgled and newly bombed.

10 Time, like an ever-rolling stream, bears all its sons away.

Exercise B

Write sentences that use words figuratively to create images to describe these items, using simile, metaphor or personification.

the sea	television
the moon	rocks
a smile	pupils running along a corridor
wind blowing across fields	a river
a sudden shock	an idea

Word building: *easily confused words*

These are words, like those you met in Unit 14, which are easily confused because they look or sound similar to each other. Check with the dictionary that you know the difference between them.

advice	advise	masterful	masterly
avenge	revenge	momentarily	momentous
draft	draught	pair pare	pear
exhausting	exhaustive	quiet	quite
imply	infer	ring	wring
imaginary	imaginative	sail	sale
informant	informer		

seam	seem	threw	through
sort	sought	vacation	vocation
stair	stare	veracious	voracious
storey	story		

Skills practice: *easily confused words*

Exercise A
Complete these sentences with the correct word chosen from the first block of paired words above (advice/advise to informant/informer).

1 My _____ tells me you were at the scene of the crime.

2 If you take my _____ you will forget everything he told you.

3 I kicked him to get my _____ for when he kicked me.

4 Does that _____ you do not trust me?

5 Grandma found such a walk absolutely _____ .

6 With the door open and the wind blowing like that, there's an enormous _____ in here.

7 You may _____ from my remarks that I do not approve.

8 There is no ghost; your fears are quite _____ .

9 The police made an _____ search of the area for clues.

10 Show me the first _____ of your story.

Exercise B

Complete these sentences with the correct word chosen from the second block of paired words (from masterful/masterly to sail/sale).

1 His performance of the piano concerto was superb; it was a _____ performance.

2 Help yourself to apples, _____ and bananas in the fruit bowl.

3 _____ I must have lost consciousness, because the next thing I knew she had gone.

4 I could do with buying a new _____ trousers in the _____ .

5 Natalie, _____ the bell for the end of school, please.

6 It was _____ a surprise when I discovered Cherie had come top.

7 Miss Goodman said the way Liz took charge of the situation was _____ but I thought she was just plain bossy.

8 The class was _____ as Mrs Ellis announced the _____ decision.

9 Dave used his penknife to _____ his apple.

10 He was so keen to _____ the secret out of me, he gave me a really hard time.

Exercise C

Complete these sentences with the correct word chosen from the third block of paired words (from seam/seem to storey/story).

1 That dog has an incredibly _____ appetite.

2 Could you mend the _____ on this dress please, Mum?

3 Our new offices are on the third floor of this ten _____ building.

4 We're taking a _____ in the United States this summer.

5 They _____ high and low for the coin, but it was never found.

6 Mrs Wright _____ the ball right over the gym roof.

7 Mark, please don't _____ out of the window.

8 You need to be really committed to the job, have a real _____ for it, if you're going to be a teacher.

9 I have looked _____ your books and only three of you have done all the work set.

10 What _____ of fool are you?

Text building: *reporting speech*

■ You have learned how to punctuate pieces of writing that contain the words that people actually use in Unit 7.

■ Reporting that someone has said something requires more than just punctuation marks. The structure of sentences often changes and some quite complex changes of verb tenses may be necessary.

1 First and second person comments are reported in the third person unless the speaker is reporting her or his own words.

For example: She says, '**I** will be home by six' becomes:
She says **she** will be home by six.

He says, '**You** have overcooked those potatoes again, John,' becomes:
He tells John that **he** has overcooked the potatoes again.

2 Usually 'that' is introduced between the introductory verb – say, tell, etc. – and the words reported.

For example: She says, 'I will be home by six' becomes:
She says **that** she will be home by six.

(Note: as in the first example above, in some cases the 'that' may be left out.)

3 When the introductory verb – say, tell, remark, etc. – is in the present or future tense, direct statements can be reported without changes of tense.

For example: She says, 'The train **will be** late' becomes:
She says that the train **will be** late.

She will tell you, 'The train **was** late' becomes:
She will tell you that the train **was** late.

4 When the introductory verb is in the past tense – which it usually is – changes are necessary to the verb form used by the speaker.

■ When the **future** was used by the speaker, this **changes to the conditional**.

For example: I said, 'Ann **will be** home next week' becomes:
I said that Ann **would be** home next week.

■ When the **future continuous** form was used by the speaker, this changes to the **conditional continuous.**

For example: I said, 'I **will be using** the car myself that evening' becomes:
I said that I **would be using** the car myself that evening.

■ When the **present** was used by the speaker, this changes to the **past**.

For example: Ella said to me, 'I never **eat** meat' becomes:
Ella said that she never **ate** meat.

■ When the **present continuous** form was used by the speaker, this changes to the **past continuous**.

For example: They said, 'We **are living** in London' becomes:
They said that they **were living** in London.

■ When the **past** form was used by the speaker, this changes to the **past perfect**, sometimes called the pluperfect or 'had' form.

For example: He said, 'I **met** her on Monday' becomes:
He said that he **had met** her on Monday.

5 **When 'this'/'these' are used by the speaker, they usually change to 'that'/'those'.**

For example: He said, 'She is coming **this** week' becomes:
He said that she was coming **that** week.

6 **Adverbs and adverbial phrases of time change in quite complex ways – as set out in this table.**

Actual words	Reported as ...
today	that day
yesterday	the day before
the day before yesterday	two days before
tomorrow	the next/following day
the day after tomorrow	in two days' time
next week/year	the following week/year
last week/year	the previous week/year
a year ago	a year before/the previous year

For example: She said, 'I saw him **the day before yesterday**'
becomes:
She said that she had seen him **two days before**.

She said, 'I'll be very busy **today**' becomes:
She said that she would be very busy **that day**.

He said, 'I'm starting work **tomorrow**' becomes:
He said that he would be starting work **the next day**.

7 **When questions are asked, the tenses of verbs change as they do with statements. 'That' is not needed and if the question begins with a question word – when, where, who, etc. – then that word is repeated in the reported question.**

For example: He asked, '**Why** didn't you put on the brake?'
becomes:
He asked **why** she/he hadn't put on the brake.

8 **If the speaker puts a question without a question word, then 'if' or 'whether' needs to be included after the introductory verb.**

For example: He asked, '**Is** anyone there?' becomes:
He asked **if/whether** anyone was there.

(Note: the question mark is no longer needed as the reported form is a statement, not a question.)

9 When commands are reported, the verb form changes to the infinitive.

For example: She said, '**Get** your coat' becomes:
She told him **to get** his coat.

(Note: commands often leave out the person spoken to and sometimes this has to be added, as in the above example. You sometimes need to change the introductory verb to a verb of 'command' or 'respect' — 'said' to 'told' above — to emphasise that the statement was an imperative.)

Skills practice

Exercise A
Change these sentences, where the introductory verb is in the present or future tense, into the reported (or indirect) speech form. Look back to the examples for help.

1 She says, 'I cannot believe it.'

2 He will say, 'My car was held up in a tail-back on the M1.'

3 Mum says, 'There is a strange lorry pulling up outside.'

4 The old woman across the street says, 'It will be wet this winter.'

5 The caretaker says, 'The school is closing down for a week.'

6 My father will say, 'Things were much better in my day.'

7 The teacher says, 'There will be no homework this evening.'

8 Richard says, 'I think Wales will win the Triple Crown.'

9 Heather will say, 'I'm sorry I forgot your birthday.'

10 She says, 'I left my umbrella in the cloakroom.'

Exercise B
Change these sentences, where the introductory verb is in the past tense, into the reported (or indirect) speech form. Look back to the examples if you need help.

1 He said, 'I am on the point of leaving'.

2 'You are as daft as my brother,' Wendy said.

3 Liam explained, 'I was going to the shops at the time.'

4 Emma declared, 'I shall go shopping.'

5 Auntie Sue said, 'I'll be coming to visit the new house.'

6 Uncle Howard said, 'I've never seen anything like it.'

7 'I have your name and address,' said the policeman.

continued ...

8 I said, 'It's very kind of you.'

9 They said, 'We always travel by public transport.'

10 'I have cleaned out the garage and given all your old toys away,' Dad said .

Exercise C

Change these sentences, which include adverbial phrases of time, into the reported (or indirect) speech form. Look at the examples for help.

1 She said, 'I'll meet you here again tomorrow.'

2 He replied, 'I will be working in Cambridge all next week.'

3 Shafiq said angrily, 'You're not having this one.'

4 Doug said, 'I passed all my exams last year.'

5 'I'm starting at university in three weeks' time,' said Rob.

6 'My aunt is coming to stay the day after tomorrow,' said Sharon.

7 Kevin said, 'I'm playing for the senior team today.'

8 Grandad said, 'I lost my glasses in town yesterday.'

9 Liz said, 'My father died a year ago today.'

10 'I shall keep these new jeans for special occasions,' said Alex.

Exercise D

Change these sentences, which include questions, into the reported (or indirect) speech form. Check back to the examples for help.

1 'Where will you spend the holidays?' asked Jenny.

2 'Is there going to be an end-of-term party?' asked Jason.

3 Jonathan said, 'Who has been borrowing my coloured pens?'

4 'Can anyone tell me the answer?' asked Miss Davies.

5 'What colour was it?' asked Maggie.

6 'Is there toast for tea?' I asked.

7 'Why did you add four eggs?' said Mrs Ahmed.

8 Dr Watson said, 'How did you know that, Holmes?'

9 'May anyone take part?' I asked.

10 'What shall we do with our wet clothes?' demanded the children.

Exercise E
Change these sentences, which include commands, into the reported (or indirect) speech form. Look back to the examples for help.

1 'Lie down at once!' he shouted.
2 'Go away!' I screamed.
3 He said, 'No one move!'
4 'Please give me another chance,' she begged.
5 'Wipe that smile off your face!' said the teacher.
6 'Stop taking so many tablets,' I advised.
7 She said, 'Say nothing about this to anyone.'
8 'Get back to your own homes!' shouted the old man.
9 'Shut the door as you go out,' the teacher said.
10 'Watch it!' I smiled.

Writing

- In a group of three, make up a short piece of dialogue about a simple everyday experience. One of you could begin to explain something that has happened and the other two could interrupt – politely! – with questions, or add further details.

- Now each of you write down the conversation in direct speech form – so keep it short.

- Next write the conversation in reported speech form, as though you were an outsider reporting the conversation to another outsider.

- When you have finished, pass one another your work and read the other two versions.

- Check how differently you have each completed this task. Can you recognise the same conversation in each report?

Unit 20: Language change

In this unit you will:

- read three extracts from travel books about Salisbury;
- learn about more figures of speech;
- learn about some more words that cause mistakes;
- practise writing.

Speaking and listening

- With a partner, read these two versions of the *Lord's Prayer*. Look carefully at the traditional version and then make a list of the following words/word forms no longer in regular use:
  - verb ending(s)
  - personal pronoun(s)
  - words/phrases/clauses no longer used in modern English.

- Discuss the changes in word forms and meaning, using the modern version to guide you, and then list any other words or word forms, not often used in modern English, that you have come across in any other texts you have read.

- Don't just think about what you have read in English; consider, for example, resource material you have come across in history, or *The Book of Common Prayer* in R.E.

Our Father in heaven,	Our Father, who art in heaven,
hallowed be your name,	hallowed be thy name;
your kingdom come,	thy kingdom come;
your will be done,	thy will be done;
on earth as in heaven.	on earth as it is in heaven.
Give us today our daily bread.	Give us this day our daily bread.
Forgive us our sins	And forgive us our trespasses,
as we forgive those who sin	as we forgive those who trespass
against us.	against us.
Save us from the time of trial	And lead us not into temptation;
and deliver us from evil.	but deliver us from evil.
For the kingdom, the power,	For thine is the kingdom,
and the glory are yours	the power, and the glory,
now and for ever. Amen.	for ever and ever. Amen.

Understanding

These three extracts give you an opportunity to look at the way similar subject matter – a visit to Salisbury in Wiltshire – may be treated over a period of time by writers with different approaches and intentions.

As a writer, novelist and merchant, Defoe travelled widely throughout Britain during the last years of the seventeenth and early years of the eighteenth centuries.

> Salisbury itself is indeed a large and pleasant city. It has two remarkable manufactures carried on in it, and which employ the poor of great part of the country round; namely, fine flannels, and long cloths for the Turkey trade, called Salisbury Whites. The people of Salisbury are gay and rich, and have a flourishing trade; and there is a great deal of good manners and good company among them; I mean, among these citizens, besides what is found among the gentlemen.
>
> The cathedral is famous for the height of its spire, which is without exception the highest, and the handsomest in England, being from the ground 410 foot, and yet the walls so exceedingly thin, that at the upper part of the spire upon a view made by the late Sir Christopher Wren, the wall was found to be less than five inches thick; upon which a consultation was had, whether the spire, or at least the upper part of it should be taken down, it being supposed to have received some damage by the great storm in the year 1703; but it was resolved in the negative, and Sir Christopher ordered it to be strengthened with bands of iron plates, as has effectually secured it; and I have heard some of the best architects say, it is stronger now than when it was first built.
>
> They tell us, this church was 40 years a-building, and cost an immense sum of money, but it must be acknowledged that the inside of the work is not answerable in the decoration of things, to the workmanship without; the painting in the choir is mean, and more like the ordinary method of common drawing room, or tavern painting, than that of a church; the carving is good, but very little of it, and it is rather a fine church than finely set off. The ordinary boast of this building, that there were as many gates as months, as many windows as days, as many marble pillars as hours in the year, is now no recommendation at all.
>
> (From *A Tour Through the Whole Island of Great Britain* by Daniel Defoe, 1724)

Cobbett, who wrote the following extract, undertook his travels as a sort of 'fact-finding mission', seeking out material for articles he wrote for his newspaper, the *Political Register.*

Yesterday morning I went into the Cathedral at Salisbury about 7 o'clock. When I got into the nave of the church, and was looking up and admiring the columns and the roof, I heard a sort of *humming,* in some place which appeared to be in the transept of the building. I found a priest and his congregation assembled. It was a parson of some sort, with a white covering on him, and five women and four men: when I arrived, there were five couple of us. I joined the congregation, until they came to the *litany;* and then, being monstrously hungry, I did not think myself bound to stay any longer. I wonder what the founders would say, if they could rise from the grave, and see such a congregation as this in this most magnificent and beautiful cathedral. I wonder what they would say, if they could know *to what purpose* the endowments of this Cathedral are now applied; and above all things, I wonder what they would say, if they could see the half-starved labourers that now minister to the luxuries of those who wallow in the wealth of those endowments. There is one thing, at any rate, that might be abstained from, by those that revel in the riches of those endowments; namely, to abuse and blackguard those of our forefathers, from whom the endowments came, and who erected the edifice, and carried so far towards the skies that beautiful and matchless spire, of which the present possessors have the impudence to boast, while they represent as ignorant and benighted creatures, those who conceived the grand design, and who executed the scientific and costly work. These fellows, in big white wigs, of the size of half a bushel, have the audacity, even within the walls of the Cathedrals themselves, to rail against those who founded them. For my part, I could not look up at the spire and the whole of the church at Salisbury, without *feeling* that I lived in degenerate times. Such a thing never could be made *now.* We *feel* that, as we look at the building, it really does appear that if our forefathers had not made these buildings, we should have forgotten, before now, what the Christian religion was!

(From *Rural Rides* by William Cobbett, 1830)

After nearly 20 years in Britain, Bill Bryson decided to move back to the United States for a time, but before leaving his much-loved home in North Yorkshire, he took a last trip around Britain, a farewell tour of the island that had been his home for so long.

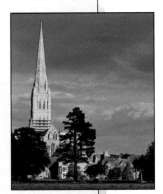

I went to Salisbury on a big red double-decker bus that swayed down winding country roads and clattered through overhanging branches in a most exciting way. I like Salisbury very much. It's just the right size for a town – big enough for cinemas and bookshops, small enough to feel friendly and livable.

Walking through the busy shopping streets now, I found it was the unattractive things that jumped out at me – Burger Kings and Prontaprints and Superdrugs and all the other manifold Enemies of the High Street, all of them with windows cluttered with announcements of special offers and all of them shoehorned into buildings without even the most fleeting nod to their character or age. In the centre of town, on a corner that ought to have been a visual pleasure, there stood a small building occupied by a Lunn Poly travel agency. Upstairs the structure was half timbered and quietly glorious; down-stairs, between outsized sheets of plate glass covered with handwritten notices of cheap flights to Tenerife and Malaga, the façade has been tiled – *tiled* – with a mosaic of multi-toned squares that looked as if they had been salvaged from a King's Cross toilet. It was just awful.

I would probably forgive Salisbury anything as long as they never mess with the Cathedral Close. There is no doubt in my mind that Salisbury Cathedral is the single most beautiful structure in England and the Close around it the most beautiful space. Every stone, every wall, every shrub is just right. It is as if every person who has touched it for 700 years has only improved it. I could live on a bench in the grounds. I sat on one now and gazed happily for a half-hour at this exquisite composition of cathedral, lawns and solemn houses.

(From *Notes from a Small Island* by Bill Bryson, 1995)

Compare these three extracts. You should comment in detail on:

- content – what each writer selects to write about;
- attitude – what each writer thinks and feels about the place;
- language – the differences in the choice of words, word forms, sentence structures etc. that each writer uses. How much have some of these changed and which are still in use today?
- purpose – what is the 'point' each writer is trying to make and how effectively has each writer communicated his ideas?

(Note: this is quite a difficult task. Think back to the discussion you and your partner had at the beginning of the unit, or work through the three extracts together, making notes before each of you writes up your answer.)

ICT Extra!

Characteristics of a webpage and an encyclopaedia entry
Print out a webpage for Salisbury and the entry from a CD encyclopaedia like 'Encarta'. In what ways are these descriptions of Salisbury different from the ones you have already considered? Think about content, attitude, language and purpose.

Learning about language: *alliteration, onomatopoeia, hyperbole, irony and rhetorical questions*

These words refer to **figures of speech** such as 'simile' that you met in the last unit.

1 **Alliteration describes the repetition of the same initial letter or sound.** It is most often used to create a particular 'sound effect', in which the sound of the words reflects the sense.

For example: 'the rustle of his sister's satin dress' not only describes the sound of the dress, but the repeated 's' sounds mirror the sound itself.

Alliteration is most popularly used to create tongue-twisters.

For example: Tommy ate a tin of tasty tinned tomatoes.

Alliteration can also be used to create amusing or memorable comments or slogans.

For example: From hell, Hull and Halifax, good Lord protect me!

(Apparently in the nineteenth century, the magistrates in Hull and Halifax had a reputation for dealing out particularly severe sentences to local criminals!)

2 **Onomatopoeia refers to a word whose sound echoes the sound it describes.** The intention, as with alliteration, is to emphasise the sound of what is being described. This may also be used to create humour.

For example: There was a loud **banging** on the door.

Suddenly the angry **buzzing** of bees disturbed the

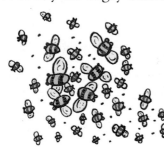

tranquil mood.
(A combination of onomatopoeia – 'buzzing' – and alliteration – the repetition of the 'b' sound.)

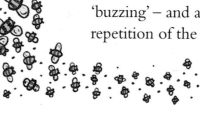

3 **Hyperbole refers to the use of huge exaggeration –** either to emphasise a point or for comic effect.

For example: I'll never be seen in that dress in a million years!

That cat was so anxious to get at the tinned salmon, I thought it would drown in its own drool! (A combination of hyperbole – 'drown' – and alliteration – the repetition of the 'd' sound.)

4 **Irony describes a statement in which one thing is said, but something different – often the opposite – is implied.** It forms the basis of much comedy, wit and satire involving sarcasm and mockery.

For example: 'But Brutus says he [Caesar] was ambitious, And Brutus is an honourable man.'

(Mark Antony in Shakespeare's *Julius Caesar*)

'I had formerly upon occasion discoursed with my master upon the nature of *government* in general, and particularly of our own *excellent Constitution*, deservedly the wonder and envy of the whole world.'

(Swift's *Gulliver's Travels*)

5 **A rhetorical question refers to a question designed to create an effect, not to find out information.** It can achieve more emphasis than a statement by posing an apparent question, but gets its effect from the assumption that there is only one possible answer.

For example: 'Who cares?'

'Here was a Caesar! When comes such another?'

(Mark Antony in Shakespeare's *Julius Caesar*)

Skills practice: *recognising alliteration, onomatopoeia, hyperbole, irony and rhetorical questions*

Exercise A

Write a short comment on each of these sentences, saying whether each contains an example of alliteration, onomatopoeia, hyperbole,

continued …

irony or a rhetorical question. Check back to the examples if you need to. Explain what effect each figure of speech creates.

1 The circus master cracked his whip as the horses circled the ring.

2 Around the rugged rock, the ragged rascal ran.

3 Who could doubt it?

4 If I've told you once, I've told you a hundred times!

5 Two tired terriers were trotting into town.

6 The satellite splashed into the sea.

7 'You call'd me dog; and for these courtesies
I'll lend you thus much moneys.'
(Shakespeare's *The Merchant of Venice*)

8 'Whereat, with blade, with bloody blameful blade,
He bravely broach'd his boiling bloody breast.'
(Shakespeare's *A Midsummer Night's Dream*)

9 'Who can be wise, amazed, temperate and furious,
Loyal and neutral, in a moment?'
(Shakespeare's *Macbeth*)

10 'All the perfumes of Arabia will not sweeten this little hand.'
(Shakespeare's *Macbeth*)

11 Are we downhearted?

12 'I did not omit even our sports and pastimes, or any other
particular which I thought might redound to the honour of
my country.'
(Swift's *Gulliver's Travels*)

13 Of course you can afford it, John; you've got tons of money!

14 The sea was slushing over the deck.

15 'How did you get into art college?'
'Usual way … failed all my exams and applied.'
(*Red Dwarf* by Grant Naylor)

Exercise B

Write sentences to create examples of alliteration, onomatopoeia, hyperbole, irony and rhetorical questions concerning:

waves/seashore	music
the sun	laughter
cliffs	fear
time	old ruins
trees	school bell

Word building: *where words come from*

Throughout this book, you have learned and constantly practised the formation of new words using a combination of the word stem plus a range of suffixes and/or prefixes. You have also learned that some of these word stems and/or prefixes and suffixes are derived from Latin or Greek words.

English has acquired words from many other sources, however.

- **Words have been adopted from other languages.**

  For example: 'shampoo', a comparatively modern word, comes from India – a Hindu word meaning 'to press'; 'mutton', a much older adoption, comes from the French word for 'sheep'.

  It is common to retain the old English noun but to use alongside it an 'adopted' adjectival form.

  For example: 'water' (noun) with the adjective of Latin/French origin 'aquatic'.

- **New words are regularly created for inventions, modern technology, new illnesses, etc. as part of the changing nature of daily life.**

  For example: 'flyover' arrived with motorways;
  'yuppie' arrived with young, prosperous executives in the City of London;
  'lunar module' arrived with space flights;
  'AIDS' arrived as a terminal illness.

- **Words may start their lives as acronyms, i.e. a word formed from the initial letters of other words.**

  For example: 'radar' originated as **RA**dio **D**etection **A**nd **R**anging (equipment).

- **Inventors, or a person associated with a particular object, may give it their name.**

  For example: 'sandwich' – the 4th Earl of Sandwich was said to have eaten only slices of bread with meat between them during long gambling and card-playing sessions.

Skills practice: *word origins*

Exercise A
Complete this table with the language of origin of the words given. You will need to use a dictionary to help you. The first one has been done for you as an example.

Word	Language of origin
sofa	Arabic
bungalow	
ketchup	
chauffeur	
algebra	
thug	
slogan	
risotto	
veranda	
canoe	
breeze	

Exercise B
Complete this table with the groups of words required. Some examples have been done to help you. Try to think of words that are comparative newcomers to the language. Remember, dictionaries provide a lot of information of this sort.

Two words formed from acronyms	**1**	NATO
	2	
Four words related to cars/motorways	**1**	underpass
	2	
	3	
	4	
Four words related to technology	**1**	
	2	byte
	3	fax
	4	
Two nouns derived from a person's name	**1**	boycott
	2	

Three words related to illness	1	
	2	paramedic
	3	

Text building: *ten common misuses of words*

1 **Using 'I' and 'me'**

■ **'I' is the first person pronoun used as subject; 'me' is the first person pronoun used as object or with prepositions.**

For example: **I (subject)** saw you.

BUT　　　　　You saw **me (object)**.
　　　　　　　Lee had lunch **with (preposition) me** on Thursday.

(Note: it is, therefore, grammatically correct to write: 'Who's that?'
'It is I.' In practice, in this particular case, however, the now commonly accepted form is: 'It is me.')

■ **When writing about yourself, it is usual to put the 'I' or 'me' after everyone else.**

For example: My sister **and I** went to the cinema.
NOT　　　　　I and my sister …

　　　　　　　My father took William, Harry **and me** out on his yacht.
NOT　　　　　My father took me, William and Harry …

2 **Using adjectives as adverbs**

In spoken English particularly, adjectives may be incorrectly used as adverbs.

For example: She sings great.
　　　　　　　We played bad.

The adjectives 'great' and 'bad' are used to describe the way the actions ('singing' and 'playing') are performed; they modify the verb, which is the job of an adverb. The correct adverbs are **'well'/'very well'** and **'badly'/'very badly'**.

3 Using comparatives and superlatives

A common error in the formation of comparatives and superlatives is to use 'more' or 'most' and also to add '-er' or '-est'.

For example: I was **more happy** than …
OR   I was **happier** than …
NOT   I was more happier than I'd ever been.

                    Tom was the **quickest** runner …
NOT   Tom was the most quickest runner in that race.

4 Using 'them' and 'these'/'those'

'Them' is a pronoun and 'these'/'those' demonstrative adjectives, so 'them' may not be used to describe something.

For example: '**these** boots' or '**those** boots'
NOT   'them boots'.

5 Using 'due to' and 'owing to'

'Due' should be used as an adjective.

For example: The bus is **due to** leave in five minutes.
                    Thanks are **due to** Mr Green, who organised
                    sports day so well.

'Owing to' is a prepositional phrase meaning 'because of'.

For example: **Owing to** the bad weather, we were delayed.

6 Using 'less' and 'fewer'

'Less' should be used only with a noun when the number of items is not an issue.

For example: I take **less** exercise than I should.

'Fewer' should be used when reference is made to the number of items (how many).

For example: I've been to **fewer** matches than usual this
                    season.
                    Ten items or **fewer**.

7 Using the infinitive

The infinitive form of a verb is the verb stem preceded by 'to' – 'to speak', 'to travel', etc.

Traditionally, it has been considered incorrect to place another word between the 'to' and the verb stem – i.e. to 'split the infinitive'.

For example: 'to go boldly …'

NOT 'to boldly go …'

Unless you want to create a specific effect, it is still probably better not to 'split the infinitive' as it can lead you into other grammatical confusions such as misplaced or unrelated phrases.

8 Using 'different'

'Different' should always be followed by the preposition 'from'. 'Different to' and 'different than' are incorrect forms sometimes used in speech.

For example: Riffat is **different from** her brothers in many ways.

NOT Riffat is different to …

9 Using 'each other' and 'one another'

'Each other' (like 'between') is used when two items are involved; 'one another' (like 'among') is used when more than two items are involved.

For example: **Two** pupils should be friendly with **each other** (just the two of them).

All the pupils should be friendly with **one another** (a whole class of them).

10 Using 'the reason why' and 'the reason is because'

In many cases, where 'why' and 'because' are used with 'the reason', they are redundant and should be left out.

For example: The reason I am lying down is I am tired.

NOT The reason why I am lying down …

NOT The reason I am lying down is because …

Skills practice: *ten common misuses of words*

Exercise A
Write out the correct version of these sentences which contain the first five types of common misuses. Check back to the examples if you need help.

1 I don't think you should talk so rough to her.
2 Glenn is the most handsomest boy I've ever met.
3 Them boots were made for walking.
4 I returned home due to the bad news.
5 Me and my friends went fishing last Tuesday.
6 On New Year's Day the weather was more worser than ever.
7 Did you see them girls from the college?
8 English has always been a problem for Adam and I.
9 Kiss me quick.
10 Pete and me are best friends.

Exercise B
Write out the correct version of these sentences which contain the second five types of common misuses. Look back to the examples if you need help.

1 My father likes to always smoke his pipe after dinner.
2 Less families go on holiday together these days.
3 The reason why I fell ill is that I picked up a virus.
4 The team looked at each other in amazement at the referee's decision.
5 The reason I dislike you is because you're selfish.
6 Alice and Sophie are very different to Jenny and Frances.
7 Paul and Mark congratulated one another on a good, clean contest.
8 Sue decided to bravely run along the dark lane.
9 Oliver's always different than the rest of us.
10 Less marks were available for the writing question.

Writing

- The task here is to write a poem.

- Remember that a poem is a very 'compact' (condensed or 'tight') piece of writing. Careful choice and positioning of words, use of a 'poetic' form and figurative language all contribute to the meaning.

- Start with a picture, a photograph or an interesting and/or unusual object to stimulate ideas. (The Art Department can usually offer helpful ideas or objects from the resources it uses for still life drawing.)

  - Look closely at your picture or object and jot down six words that describe what you see.

  - Think about the purpose of the object or what people in the picture are doing and jot down six more words.

  - Think about how your senses – what you can see, hear, smell, taste and touch – might respond and jot down any more words and phrases that occur to you.

  - Check back through your notes and sort out words and phrases that go together. Discard those that are irrelevant.

  - Try to turn some of your words and phrases into similes or other figures of speech.

  - Organise your groups of words or ideas into some sort of order.

  - Using a 'free verse' form, make a first draft of your poem.

  - Look again at your stimulus material, focus on what exactly you want to say about it and see how far your first draft reflects this.

  - Revise your draft, cutting out unnecessary words, re-arranging lines and word order to improve the effect. Consider whether using rhyme would help.

  - Re-draft your poem, and repeat the last two stages until you have produced a final version you are happy with.

Unit 21: Review: the final check

In this unit you will:

- plan assessment work for speaking and listening;
- review how to demonstrate understanding;
- read two sonnets by Shakespeare;
- review what you have learned about grammar, spelling and punctuation;
- learn consciously to craft your work to achieve its purpose.

Speaking and listening: *assessing achievement*

Throughout the course, your teacher will have assessed your performance in speaking and listening skills. This will have involved a range of speaking and listening activities.

- Working with a partner, check back through all the Speaking and listening units and note the different types of speaking activity you have taken part in – for example, pairs work, group discussion, role plays, delivering a talk – using speech to persuade, to inform, to investigate, to entertain, etc.

- Decide where you felt least confident and then plan any additional assessment items you can put to your teacher to improve your level of attainment.

Understanding: *checking what you have understood*

Remind yourself of the ways in which you have learned to approach texts to show your understanding of and response to what you have read.

- **Focus on the basic facts or ideas**
  What information is being put across? What are you learning – about people, things, ideas – from this piece of writing?

- **Focus on the purpose of the writing**
  What are the writer's intentions? To inform? To persuade? To entertain? etc.

- **Focus on the intended reader**

  Who does the writer have in mind in writing this? Who/what is the intended audience?

- **Focus on what is implied about attitudes or feelings**

  Why does the author/a character say that? What tone of voice would be used for such a statement?

- **Focus on the language and structure of the writing**

  Why does the writer make this happen? Why are these words chosen? Why are things arranged in this order? What are the implications of this figurative use of language? What is the effect of using these grammatical constructions, verb forms, etc.? What emphasis has been achieved by using punctuation in this way?

Check you can handle all these skills by looking at these two Shakespeare sonnets.

(Note: this is not an easy assignment, so to begin with, work with a partner, discussing the meaning of each sonnet, looking up words you do not know in a dictionary and making sure you understand exactly what is being said. You may find it helpful to make notes as you go along, as preparation for the question that follows.)

The sonnet is a traditional form for a love poem. It consists of just 14 lines, with usually ten syllables in a line, and conforms to various rhyming patterns. In this case, the first 12 lines rhyme alternately in three groups of four lines; the last two lines rhyme with each other.

Sonnet 18

Shall I compare thee to a summer's day?
Thou art more lovely and more temperate.
Rough winds do shake the darling buds of May,
And summer's lease hath all too short a date;
Sometime too hot the eye of heaven shines,
And often is his gold complexion dimm'd;
And every fair from fair sometimes declines,
By chance or nature's changing course untrimm'd;
But thy eternal summer shall not fade
Nor lose possession of that fair thou owest;
Nor shall Death brag thou wander'st in his shade,
When in eternal lines to time thou growest.
   So long as men can breathe or eyes can see,
   So long lives this and this gives life to thee.

Sonnet 130

My mistress' eyes are nothing like the sun;
Coral is far more red than her lips' red;
If snow be white, why then her breasts are dun;
If hairs be wires, black wires grow on her head.
I have seen roses damask'd red and white,
But no such roses see I in her cheeks;
And in some perfumes is there more delight
Than in the breath that from my mistress reeks.
I love to hear her speak, yet well I know
That music hath a far more pleasing sound;
I grant I never saw a goddess go;
My mistress, when she walks, treads on the ground.
    And yet, by heaven, I think my love as rare
    As any she belied with false compare.

Compare these two sonnets. You should comment in detail on:

■ the theme of each;

■ the language in which Shakespeare expresses his different ideas in the two sonnets;

■ which one you prefer.

Learning about language: *checking grammatical terms*

You have learned a lot of grammatical terms as you have worked through this book, but simply 'knowing the words' does not have a lot of value in itself. The important thing is that you understand the different grammatical forms and structures and their functions; the correct terminology helps you discuss clearly and accurately what you read and write.

■ However, as a check on your familiarity with some of the terms – and a reminder that in some cases you may need to refresh your memory on some points – read this passage, the opening paragraph of David Park's short story *Oranges from Spain*, and complete the table that follows.

■ The first one has been done as an example.

I was sixteen years old and very young when I went to work for Mr Breen in his fruit shop. It was that summer when it seemed to rain every day and a good day stood out like something special. I got the job through patronage. My father and Gerry Breen went back a long way – that always struck me as strange, because they were so unlike as men. Apparently, they were both born in the same street and grew up together, and even when my father's career as a solicitor took him up-market, they still got together occasionally. My father collected an order of fruit every Friday night on his way home from work, and as children we always talked about 'Gerry Breen's apples'. It's funny the things you remember, and I can recall very clearly my mother and father having an argument about it one day. She wanted to start getting fruit from the supermarket for some reason, but my father wouldn't hear of it. He got quite agitated about it and almost ended up shouting, which was very unlike him. Maybe he acted out of loyalty, or maybe he owed him some kind of favour, but whatever the reason, the arrangement continued.

personal pronoun as subject of a sentence	I
proper noun	
demonstrative pronoun	
main clause	
preposition	
verb phrase	
co-ordinating conjunction	
subordinate clause	
plural noun	
adjective	
subordinating conjunction	
possessive pronoun (determiner)	
abstract noun	
modal verb	
verb in simple past	
verb infinitive	

Word building: *checking word building*

You have learned how to combine word stems with suffixes and/or prefixes to create words with different grammatical forms. You have learned some of the rules that govern spelling, and something about how new words enter the language.

Review all these word building skills in the following three exercises, which will help you check what you know – in an entertaining way!

Exercise A

Invent words for the following. You can use foreign words/prefixes/suffixes, acronyms, inventors' names etc. Some suggestions have been made to help you.

BAnana and BLACKberry pie	bablack pie
an automatic board cleaner	
to take lessons at home	telelearn
machine that translates cat/dog speech	
device to rouse inattentive pupils	
to make excuses for not doing homework	
impossibly small handwriting	microscript
someone who always arrives late	to (someone's name?)
a pupil who knows nothing of maths	
a clockwork-driven car	
a badger tunnel under a road	
elastic guy ropes for a tent	
someone who writes with their left hand	
to sneeze very loudly	to exnasalode

Exercise B

Here's a list of 15 words, all of which are wrongly spelt. Write the correct versions and then check with a dictionary. If you have made mistakes, look back at the rules and make sure you understand them.

grafitti	
skillful	
freind	
conceed	
merryment	
terrifyed	
employible	
appealling	
conterfiet	
marvelous	
advantagous	
wholey	

comfortabley	
pleasureable	
encouragment	

Text building: *checking punctuation rules*

Sentences markers – capital letters and usually full stops – are essential to composition and grammar.

All other punctuation marks are used for convenience of reading. Their main purpose is:

- to 'phrase' the sentence, showing at a glance the relationships of its various parts
- to indicate the tone of the voice – for example, in questions or exclamations
- to give emphasis and make clear precisely what the writer is trying to say.

The well punctuated sentence is therefore simply one whose meaning and construction the reader can grasp with the minimum of effort.

Here is a piece of writing completely without punctuation. Rewrite it, adding punctuation and identifying any points at which meaning might change according to the punctuation used.

Mike and Michelle were sitting at home one evening planning to enter their pet snails Les and Lily for the snail Derby now then Les said Mike to his favourite gastropod youre my favourite gastropod I thought I was your favourite said Michelle but youre not a gastropod now then youre going with Lily to the mollusc Derby next Friday evening dont speak to me like that said Michelle I wasnt said Mike I was talking to Les when there was a loud knock at the door oh dear said Mike as he stood up Ive trodden on Lily thats our chance of winning the mollusc Derby gone for another year.

Writing

■ **Before you start to write anything, remember that a writer is a craftsman who works with words – and punctuation – to create a text with meaning.** Words do not just happen on the page; they are the result of a conscious process of thinking, planning, organising and choosing by you, the writer. So exercise your craftsmanship with all the care of an artist composing a picture.

■ **Who are you writing for?** In most cases, what you write will be seen by your teacher and perhaps no one else. Nevertheless, it is important to know the intended purpose and audience of your work so that you choose an appropriate form and tone for your writing. Are you writing a story? Are you putting forward a point of view? Are you presenting a report? A speech to your class will have different requirements from a story for the Year 3 pupils at your local primary school. Whatever subject matter or content you choose, your audience will affect your choice of words, the shape and complexity of your sentences and the way you link ideas together.

■ **How will you organise your material?** If you are writing a story, what characters will you create? What will you make happen to them to bring out their personalities and show the reader what they are like? If you are communicating ideas, what is the most important point you want to get across? What order will you choose for events or ideas?

■ **What role will you adopt?** Will the story be told in the first person – as though you witnessed everything? Or in the third person – you standing outside events, but seeing and knowing everything? What will be the effect of these different approaches? What would be the effect of an account in the second person?

■ **How can you catch your reader's interest with an effective opening?** If you are writing a non-narrative piece (a discussion or report), what will your reader be most anxious to know? What intriguing or original approach will engage your reader so you may get your thoughts across – especially if your subject has been dealt with many times or by many other writers?

■ **How can you link your material to maintain the reader's interest or provide guidance through a complex argument?** What effects may be achieved by using paragraphs of different length? What contribution can a variety of sentence structures make? Can you use, say, pronouns to help your material hang together – give it cohesion – to avoid repetition? Can you use a variety of phrases and subordinate clauses to develop sentences in interesting and different ways?

■ **How will your use of verbs contribute to the tone and impact of your writing?** What use will you make of the more impersonal passive voice compared with the less formal active voice? Will you use any imperatives – possibly more forceful – or conditional/subjunctive forms – more tentative and showing deference? Will you write in the present tense or mainly use the past? How will the choice of tense affect the impact of what you say? Have you chosen an appropriate tense for the sort of writing task you are working on?

■ **How will your choice of vocabulary affect the impact of your work?** Do you need vigorous verbs to carry forward an action-packed narrative? Or do you need more complex technical language to convey difficult ideas? Is the language you choose for the people in a narrative appropriate to their characters? Is the language you choose suitable for the task and your audience? Can you use figures of speech to give vividness, emphasis or humour to your writing?

■ **Have you used your knowledge of grammar to communicate your meaning clearly and accurately?** Are the forms of words used grammatically correct and suitable for their purpose? Where you have used different grammatical forms of words, have you spelt them accurately? Where you have added prefixes and suffixes to word stems, have you formed the words correctly?

■ **Can punctuation help to convey your meaning?** Does it help the reader to follow the shape of your sentences and/or any dialogue you use? Can it be used to give further indication of the ways characters speak or think?

■ **All these elements contribute to the creation and crafting of your work.**

- At this point, you will write a first draft.

- You will then revise this and repeat the process as many times as you think necessary until you have a piece of writing as well crafted as a piece of sculpture.

- Finally, you will proof-read it one last time to eliminate 'slips of the pen' – and your masterpiece will be complete!

The final task

■ Review the work in your portfolio of material for teacher assessment.

■ Look back at some of the pieces of written work you have completed as you have worked your way through this textbook. Which ones please you most? Could they be improved in the light of more recent knowledge and experience?

■ You have re-worked some pieces already. Are there some pieces which seem poor, but which you now see have potential? How could these be developed?

■ The choice is yours! Take one piece of work and give it all the 'craftsmanship' you can.

Index